Norwich T

Exploring Life With N

~Tales of Love, Learning, Laughter, and Loss~

Barbara E. Huffman

All photos by Michael & Barbara Huffman

This book is dedicated to my sweet Divot, whose passing so completely broke my heart I was compelled to finally finish what I had started. I miss you every day Divie Dog.

"The only cure for grief is action."
George Henry Lewis

ISBN-13: 978-0-9850041-0-1

Cover photography and design by Michael Huffman

CONTENTS

ACKNOWLEDGEMENTS

Much love and thanks to my husband and best friend Michael, for your encouragement and help in pursuing this very personal, and sometimes very painful journey. Your kindness, caring, immense compassion, and creative input have been invaluable.

A big thank you to Magda Omansky for your help in editing this book and for helping me to keep the message focused.

Thanks and appreciation to my friend Carol Wilcox for encouraging me to take a leap of faith and write. Thank you too for all of your advice!

Thanks to friends Pat, Claudia, and Cathryn for your endless enthusiasm and encouragement.

Thanks to all the kind people who have visited the Norwich Tales website over the years. Your love for Nigel and Divot, and your desire to learn more about the Norwich Terrier breed has made it a fun and gratifying labor of love!

Thank you to Carol and Fran for giving us the opportunity to explore life with Norwich Terriers in the first place. Nigel and Divot have meant the world to us.

Thank you Dr. Bart Bryan D.V.M., and Dr. Bob Bergman D.V.M., for contributing information for this book. Your love for animals is evident in the way you care for them.

Much applause and appreciation for all the hobby breeders who tirelessly strive to improve, and fiercely protect this very special, very charming breed.

FORWARD

We make deep connections with our dogs. Barb Huffman's story is both personal and universal. It is a book for Norwich Terrier lovers, for "terrier people", for "dog people", really for anyone with a heart for a pet and curiosity about one dog breed's characteristics.

The Norwich Terrier, a relatively rare breed with scant literature devoted to it, is the main character of the book. Without preaching, Barb Huffman delivers a down-to-earth manual for living with and understanding this breed. Exemplified by anecdotes about her male dog Nigel and her female Divot, the author's story extrapolates the private events into more common truths: "teachable moments" in Barb's own words. Whether you are a seasoned fancier of the breed, a novice Norwich Terrier owner, or a dog lover at large, you will equally enjoy this wonderful tale and learn a thing or two.

One may ask why anyone would narrow their pet ownership to one dog breed. Is one breed of dog that much different than the next one? Let us back up for a moment. For thousands of years, our human history was intertwined with the domesticated dog, even argued by authors like Dr. Stanley Coren to be dependant on that connection. This relationship became even stronger when humans figured out that they could selectively breed dogs for particular traits. And did they ever! While today millions of Americans find their lives more fulfilling by sharing their lives with a family dog, many pet owners under-appreciate how particularized each breed of dog really is.

To understand the breadth and depth of idiosyncrasies in any one breed of dog one needs to look no further than the wide physical pluralism between canines. There is no denying the vast differences between a Great Dane and a Chihuahua. Those physical differences, shaped by generations of dogs selectively bred for particular traits, are but a tiny part of the whole story. A handbook like this one, devoted to living with one particular dog breed, is valuable.

It is easy to forget that even a young breed like the Norwich Terrier collectively shares specific traits not found in that same arrangement of features in any other dogs. And without taking anything away from each dog's individuality, the breed's distinguishing characteristics shape their temperaments, needs, and the core of who they are. To capture that essence and understand it can only contribute to a better dog ownership.

I have never met Barb Huffman in person, yet I feel a close connection with the author of this book through a common experience of loving Norwich Terriers. Any dog owner who reads this heart-felt autobiographical tale of the joys and sorrows of living with a terrier breed will undoubtedly feel equally connected. Barb Huffman has succeeded in pouring out her heart onto the pages you are holding, all the while remaining faithful to her goal of writing an educational book about living with the Norwich Terrier.

Magda Omansky,
Freelance dog writer and Norwich Terrier breeder

INTRODUCTION

I want to begin by saying that I am not an expert on the Norwich Terrier breed, or an expert on canine behavior. I'm not even a writer. I'm just *writing.*

That is who I am not. Who I *am,* is a dog lover who has a special love and affection for this lovable, quirky breed: the Norwich Terrier. This is the story of my journey of learning, and an honest account of my failures and victories with my dogs. When I finally did get the dog of my dreams I did some things right (a few), did some things wrong (many), but I never stopped trying to find the key to living successfully with my dogs. Maybe it could be said that my expertise lies in learning from my mistakes. Some of the experiences I share may cause you to cringe at my complete lack of understanding about dogs in the early days, and some experiences may make you laugh. It is my sincere hope that something you read here will be of help to you as you search for the perfect dog, and then bring him or her into your home to live.

The book is divided into two sections. Part 1 is about the Norwich Terrier breed, including history, health, and how to tell a good breeder from a bad one. Part 2 is about life with my Norwich Terriers, Nigel and Divot. Each chapter of Part 2 also contains Teachable Moments where I share something that I learned about how to solve a particular behavioral problem (many of which I helped create), or a learning experience that enhanced my bond with my dogs, and made me a more informed dog owner. Woven in are of course *Norwich Tales*, personal stories and observations of my quirky little Norwich Terriers. These moments – all true – span puppyhood through the golden years. Nigel and Divot are the message. I am the messenger.

For ease of reading, when speaking of dogs in a general sense, I tend to use the masculine pronoun "he." It is just easier than saying, "he *or* she" constantly. No offense intended!

One beautiful day in the fall of 1998 when my puppy Nigel was about 6 months old, we were outside working in the yard. I left him at the side of the house and went to the garage to fetch a tool. As I was walking toward the garage, I noticed a butterfly drifting by, and thought it was unusual to see one so late in the year, especially in Michigan. When I returned to the side of the house where I had left Nigel, there I found him eagerly waiting for me, with only a wing of the once beautiful butterfly sticking out of his mouth. He had never shown the slightest interest in hunting *anything* but apparently the butterfly had suddenly brought out his terrier instincts. While I was somewhat disheartened that he had killed such a beautiful and delicate creature, I had to laugh. He was so cute and so eager to show me his prize! I wanted to share the silly tale with someone who would appreciate the sweet humor of the moment. In June of 2001, when Divot came into our lives, there were even more charming Norwich tales to tell.

My husband Michael suggested the creation of a website, where I could share stories about life with Norwich Terriers, and share some of the many photos we had taken of Nigel and Divot. After all, while we were waiting for *our* puppy, looking at photos, searching for websites, and reading about dogs helped soothe our impatient spirits. Our friend Donnie Fischer, a talented young web designer, took the website idea and ran with it. In spring of 2002, Norwich Tales the website was born (www.norwichtales.com). Donnie built a series of beautiful websites for Norwich Tales, turning Nigel and Divot into household names in some Norwich Terrier circles. Over the years, as the website continued to evolve, many faithful visitors suggested that I write a book about my experiences with Nigel and Divot, a subject which I am clearly passionate about. So, here we are.

If you are searching for the right dog for you and your family, and it is not a Norwich Terrier, this book may still be of interest to you. I hope to provoke thoughts to help you determine whether a Norwich Terrier, or *any* dog is right for you, right now. Sharing your life with a dog requires a great deal time and effort, it is definitely expensive, it can be incredibly fun, and it will certainly break your heart. It is not for everyone.

I have had a great deal of fun and many laughs with Nigel and Divot, have had some frustrating times, and sad times too, but I have always had 100% love and devotion to them. Nigel and Divot have allowed me to enter a very magical, wonderful, and whimsical world.

Join me as we explore life with Norwich Terriers.

Part I - Chapter 1

Breed History, Description, and Health

LONG AGO IN A LAND FAR, FAR AWAY

Norwich Terriers originated in England and were developed from several terriers of the day, to be ratters in the barns of English farms. These predecessors to our modern day Norwich Terriers probably had Yorkshire and Irish Terriers in their genetic background, as well as other terriers of the day. In the early days as they continued to evolve, these small, game little terriers were called Cantab Terriers, Jones Terriers and sometimes, Trumpington Terriers. At one point a man known as "Roughrider Jones" is said to have become a breeder and dealer of these small terriers in the area of Norwich England. Most sources give Jones credit for naming the breed "the Norwich Terrier."

These fearless, driven, hardy little terriers were kept in packs and were efficient at their tasks – ridding barns and land of vermin. They also proved effective at flushing out foxes during the hunt. Proving themselves as effective "verminators," the ancestor of the modern day Norwich Terrier became a popular choice of 1880s Cambridge students to keep their vermin population in check. Perhaps this was their first foray into being "house dogs."

The word Terrier is derived from the Latin word "Terra" which means, "earth." Terriers are called "earth dogs" for their excellent, natural digging abilities and willingness to go to ground after prey. The Norwich Terrier's short, strong legs, along with a harsh, wiry coat that easily sheds dirt, water, and debris, are perfect assets for such an activity. Form follows function. They were born to dig.

The closest cousin to the Norwich Terrier is the Norfolk Terrier. The first most noticeable difference between the two breeds is the ears. The Norwich has prick ears (think: witches hat) and the Norfolk has drop, or folded ears, but the difference does not stop there. Those who know both breeds well, say that the Norwich has a "softer temperament" than the Norfolk. When I asked a 34 year veteran Norwich and Norfolk breeder about the differences between the two breeds, she describes the differences like this: "Norfolks *want* you and Norwich *need* you. My Norwich want to be on top of me, and the Norfolks want to be next to me." She adds, "Norfolks are problem solvers, and I find them to be more intelligent and independent. This is of course, for the most part." While being very similar in size and appearance, they are very different breeds.

The Norwich Terrier was recognized by the American Kennel Club (AKC) in 1936. Both the prick ear and drop eared dogs were considered the same breed and were shown together in conformation, but in 1979, the Norwich and Norfolk Terriers were officially separated into two distinct breeds by the AKC. The National Breed club followed suit 30 years later and split into two separate clubs in 2009. This has allowed each club to focus on the individual issues concerning these very different breeds.

Though they possess a dual nature of both determined and fearless hunter, and loyal people lover, modern Norwich Terriers have become most valued for their companionship.

GETTING MORE SPECIFIC

A breed standard is a written description of the ideal for the breed. According to the official breed standard, "The Norwich Terrier, spirited and stocky with sensitive prick ears and a slightly foxy expression, is one of the smallest working terriers. This sturdy descendent of ratting companions, eager to dispatch small vermin alone or in a pack, has good bone and substance and an almost weatherproof coat. The ideal *height* should not exceed 10 inches tall at the withers…*weight* approximately 12 pounds. It should be in proportion to the individual dog's structure and balance." Regarding the Norwich Terrier's head, the standard reads, "A slightly foxy expression. Eyes, small dark and oval shaped with black rims... Ears medium size and erect. Set well apart with pointed tips." The Norwich Terrier's coat is described in the standard as, "Hard, wiry and straight, lying close to the body with a definite undercoat." Norwich Terrier colors are, "All shades of red, wheaten, black & tan, or grizzle. White marks are not desirable." The official breed standard describes the temperament of the Norwich Terrier as "Gay, fearless, loyal, and affectionate. Adaptable and sporting, they make ideal companions."[1] For the complete and official breed standard, visit the Norwich Terrier Club of America (NTCA) website at www.norwichterrierclub.org.

HEALTH CONCERNS IN THE NORWICH TERRIER

When I first began researching the breed in 1994, the main health concerns being discussed were luxating patellas and collapsing trachea, but now unfortunately, the Norwich Terrier like so many other breeds has added additional health problems to its list of concerns.

In recent years, along with collapsing trachea, more respiratory related conditions have appeared in the breed. These individual respiratory ailments include: collapsing trachea, narrow trachea, elongated soft palate, enlarged tonsils, and everted laryngeal saccules (ELS). These respiratory disorders are collectively referred to as Upper Airway Syndrome (UAS). In her article *The Anatomy of Upper Airway Syndrome*, the NTCA Health Chair, says, "UAS is not a static problem, but rather a condition that can worsen in time, as one anatomic abnormality causes deformation elsewhere. I find the dynamic nature of the condition crucial to understanding UAS, but regrettably, this is the most ignored fact of the UAS. Diagnosing a dog as 'mildly affected' at the age of two, for example does not mean that he will stay that way for life… So, please think of UAS as a *chronic* condition. No matter how successful a particular corrective surgery might be, it is never a permanent fix."[2]

Epilepsy can also be found in the Norwich Terrier breed. "Epilepsy is the most common neurological symptom veterinarians encounter. Between 0.5 and 5.7 percent of all dogs, including mixed breeds, experience seizures in their lifetime, with reported incidence slightly higher among males than females ... Primary (idiopathic, genetic, true or inherited) epilepsy is probably caused by a chemical defect within the brain cells, although no known cause can be demonstrated through diagnostic tests currently available. Some researchers believe idiopathic canine epilepsy has strong genetic mechanisms... Secondary (acquired or symptomatic) epilepsy is the result of damage to the brain cells from one or more of a myriad of causes. Metabolic disorders involving the liver or thyroid gland; intracranial diseases such as encephalitis; brain tumors; traumas to the head and toxic reactions to flea preventives and vegetation sprays have all been implicated..." [3]

Some Norwich Terriers can be sensitive to vaccines, especially the Leptospirosis vaccine. These dogs may experience anaphylactic shock – a systemic allergic reaction to the vaccine. For some dogs, anaphylactic shock can be overcome with emergency treatment, but for others, the result is death. Some dogs can suffer an autoimmune response to the rabies vaccine, called Rabies Vaccine Induced Ischemic Dermatopathy (RVI-ID). While not lethal, it can lead to discomfort and can disfigure the dog. Treatment is long-term and can be expensive.

Allergies have become more common in the modern dog world, and unfortunately no breed is immune. Some environmental allergies can be seasonal as with people. A dog who suffers from an environmental allergy will have itchy skin, especially the feet. While not life threatening, skin allergies can make a dog miserable, and excessive licking and scratching can lead to sores, which can then lead to infections. Some dogs are sensitive to certain food ingredients. It is believed (at least by the holistic veterinarians I have spoken to), that the use of inexpensive filler ingredients in some commercial dog foods causes many dogs to suffer from digestive upsets as well as itchy skin.

The sad truth is that no breed, or combination of breeds is immune to health problems. To that end, when you work with a dedicated Norwich Terrier breeder who takes the health of the breed seriously, you will find that they test any dog they plan to breed for clearances on eyes, hips, and patellas. These are the tests recommended by the Norwich Terrier Club of America as of the date of this writing. The results for eye tests are registered with an open database at Canine Eye Registration Foundation (CERF), and for hips and knees, at Orthopedic Foundation for Animals (OFA). Dogs having these three tests performed appear in one, all-inclusive database on the Canine Health Information Center (CHIC) website so that other breeders, as well as potential buyers can easily access the information. See Resources section at the end of this book for the website listings for these databases. There are never any guarantees, but in her article *What's the Deal with Health Tests?* NTCA Health Chair, Magda Omansky reports "Norwich Terriers born between the years 2000 and 2002, and entered into OFA, showed 15.7% of hip dysplasia among 121 dogs tested. Just in the next couple of years that number dropped to 8.2% based on 97 dogs tested." She goes on to say, "I know that many breeding decisions were influenced by what we could learn in OFA database."[4]

With the information found in the database, concerned breeders were able to make much more informed decisions on breeding stock they chose, and the numbers proved it. Responsible breeders test *before* they breed! Health testing is expensive and only a truly responsible, dedicated breeder will do it, and then make the choice to breed *only* their healthy dogs. This indicates a sincere desire to improve the breed by making informed decisions. Their goal is a healthy dog with the correct temperament, not the production of puppies for sale. These hobby breeders are the opposite of the puppy mill. We will explore this topic in depth in a later chapter.

Last but certainly not least, is a health concern that is preventable – obesity. This particular health problem is one that became very personal to me, as by the time Nigel was two years old, he was approximately four pounds overweight and considered obese. An overweight dog is an unhealthy dog. Not only does obesity prevent your dog from moving comfortably and having normal stamina, but carrying too much weight is hard on your dog's structure and organ systems. Obesity increases the risk of diabetes, heart disease, and high blood pressure. Obese dogs can also suffer from respiratory difficulties, and for dogs with already compromised breathing, it can exacerbate the problem. Monitoring your dog's weight is part of your responsibility as a dog owner. If he is overweight it is because he is either overindulged with treats, overfed at mealtimes, not eating an appropriate diet, not getting enough exercise, or a combination of some of the above. If your dog is overweight and not being overfed and under exercised, have a physical with blood work done to rule out disease. Norwich Terriers are tenacious dogs, and this means they beg with the same tenacity with which they hunt. I will go into more depth on this topic in Chapter 6.

The Norwich Terrier Club of America (NTCA) is working to educate the public on health issues concerning the Norwich Terrier and is putting its resources toward finding the genetic keys to some of these illnesses but that takes time, patience, the honesty of breeders and owners, and of course, money.

Chapter 2
Is This The Right Breed For Me?

QUESTIONS YOU MUST ASK YOURSELF

Now that you know a brief history of the Norwich Terrier as a small, pack oriented vermin hunter, how does this knowledge of the past affect your present decision about this breed? Your willingness to think about the following questions will help you to discern whether a Norwich Terrier, or *any* dog is right for you.

"Is a Norwich Terrier the right breed for me?"
That depends. Just because the Norwich Terrier is a small dog, it does not necessarily mean that this is the right breed for you just because you have a "small dog" in mind. Currently there are 27 AKC recognized terrier breeds, and it is said that of all of them, the Norwich Terrier has the softest temperament. This generally means that while the Norwich is a fearless hunter, he is submissive to people. Historically kept as a pack terrier, he gets along well with most other dogs, especially other Norwich Terriers in my experience. The Norwich Terrier does however have the same tenacity, feistiness, and attitude of his larger brethren. The small, sturdy Norwich is not fine boned like a toy breed of similar size, and the coat is coarse, hard, and wiry. A Norwich with a proper coat can feel very much like a Brillo pad – not at all soft to the touch. Norwich Terriers are by nature inquisitive, intelligent, and energetic little dogs. They have a fun sense of humor, and a quirky personality. While they are very affectionate, most are not likely to be *just* a lap dog. Norwich Terriers need regular exercise and mental stimulation along with lap time. They do not thrive being left alone for long periods of time.

"How time consuming is a dog?"
A dog is a very time consuming pet. They require some form of exercise, grooming, and playtime every day. Training begins the moment you get your puppy and it is something that will continue and evolve over the life of your dog.

Dogs are social creatures. Leaving a dog alone for long periods of time can sometimes result in behavioral problems stemming from boredom, frustration, or even fear. Some of these types of problems can be eliminated by regular, age-appropriate exercise before leaving your dog home alone. If your work takes you away all day, you may want to consider getting someone trustworthy to check on your dog. This will give him some company, some playtime, and allow him to relieve himself once or twice during the day. Because the Norwich is an energetic and sometimes, busy little dog, he may not always be content to lie on your lap while you try to relax after a long day of work, especially a younger dog. A morning and additional evening walk will be very much appreciated and likely necessary for your Norwich to "get the wiggles out." You can sometimes substitute a walk with an energetic game of fetch or other activity that gets him moving. Without enough human interaction and daily exercise, you could wind up with a frustrated and pudgy pet. Neither of you will be happy.

The Bottom Line? Make sure you have the necessary amount of time to spend with a dog to satisfy his needs. If you do not have the time or will not make the time, please consider another type of pet.

"Does it really matter what a dog was originally bred for?"
Too often people buy a breed of dog for every reason but the right one. They like the look or the size of the dog, or the way the coat feels, or they like the status of the breed. While we all make our decisions about what kind of dog we want based on some type of attraction, do not overlook knowing and understanding one of the most important things about your potential dog: *What was he bred to do?*

Norwich Terriers were bred to hunt vermin. This instinct enables them to think and act very quickly, without the need of human instruction to get their job done. While your Norwich Terrier's primary duties would most likely be that of companion, not ridding your home and land of vermin, the hunting instinct is still deeply ingrained in this breed. This means that you cannot get upset and discipline him when he proudly presents you with a cute baby bunny he's just killed. Bred to hunt vermin – even go to ground for it – the Norwich Terrier has excellent digging abilities, speed, courage, and tenacity. Instincts and genetics are powerful forces! While some people might find it a bit difficult to live with a terrier, others find it an exciting, humorous experience.

Divot with a muzzle full of dirt after a digging episode.

The Bottom Line? Know what a dog was bred for and fully embrace it or keep searching for a breed that better suits your needs and wants. If you really have your heart set on a low energy lap dog, this mighty little hunter is not for you. If you have a home with other pets such as a Guinea pig, rabbit, hamster or other pocket pets, it would *not* be advisable to choose a Norwich Terrier!

"Do small dogs need exercise?"
Certainly!

The Bottom Line? Every dog needs age and health appropriate exercise.

"I have a fenced in yard. Isn't that enough?"

A fenced in yard is a necessity for your dog's safety and containment, and for ease of potty outings, but if that yard is your dog's only outing, you are denying him some things that are very important to a dog: socialization and exploration. Your dog needs the mental stimulation of exploring the world both inside and outside the fence with you. Our domestic dogs' ancestors were roaming canids, which makes our dogs natural born rovers (pun intended). Their wild cousins still walk their territories, looking for food and marking their territorial boundaries. A leash-walk with your dog heeling at your side, trained not to pull or lunge, will not only keep him safe, but will also reinforce your role as his leader, and protector. A well-socialized dog can then be included in other social activities such as visiting friends and relatives, lunch at an outdoor café, shopping, and even vacationing!

Nigel happily runs at a fenced in park.

The Bottom Line? Every dog needs social interaction. Including your dog in activities outside of your home and yard will enhance his life and strengthen your bond.

"Do I really want a dog I cannot trust off-leash?"
Make sure that you are willing to provide safety and containment for your Norwich Terrier. For the most part they have a high prey drive. Should the opportunity to give chase to perceived prey present itself, most Norwich will seize the moment. Besides a high prey drive, Norwich Terriers are friendly dogs, and a neighbor walking by could be enough to send him running to the street to say hello, putting his life in danger. Also, being small dogs, Norwich Terriers are vulnerable to larger dogs that may be left to roam free. Wild predators are certainly a threat to our domestic dogs. While a fence is not a guarantee of safety, (especially from wild predators) it is a necessity for every day safety and convenience. It is your responsibility to protect your dog, and not allow him to be a nuisance to neighbors.

The Bottom Line? If you cannot or are not willing to provide the security of a fenced yard, and you aren't willing to take your dog out on a leash for every outing, you should consider a breed other than a Norwich Terrier. While some Norwich owners do allow their dogs off leash, each time they do so, there is a risk. Being able to trust a Norwich Terrier off-leash comes after much training time.

"What is my skill level for training a dog?"
Norwich Terriers are intelligent dogs and some can be strong-willed. This is not to say they are not obedient and highly trainable, but you must find the right method of training and communicating with your individual dog, keeping him interested in your efforts. In my opinion, there is no "one size

fits all" method for dog training. Most training classes are affordable but if you want one-on-one training for your dog, it can be expensive, but definitely worth it if you have a specific problem(s) you want to address. Are you willing to seek out the help of a professional trainer or behaviorist if necessary?

The Bottom Line? Training your Norwich Terrier takes patience, creativity, and a willingness to be flexible and adaptable to his temperament and abilities. Be honest about your own abilities and the time you have available for putting in the hard work of training. Hiring a trainer can be pricey but beneficial.

"Is the Norwich Terrier a 'barky' little dog?"
My experience has been no, they are not prone to senseless barking. All dogs bark – that's natural. When a dog runs around barking for no reason, that's *not* natural. A dog that barks for no reason is possibly bored, frustrated, or may be fearful. Some things that will cause most dogs to bark are: 1) Someone is at the door; 2) playing, chasing, and wrestling; 3) there is a critter in the yard; 4) to signal that he needs to go out to relieve himself. All of these occasions are perfectly normal reasons to bark.

The Bottom Line? If you cannot tolerate noise in your home for some reason (baby sleeping, home office, etc.) and you are not willing to provide your dog with a physical and mental outlet and proper training, you should consider a different type of pet. All dogs bark!

"Are Norwich Terriers good with children?"
Norwich Terriers generally love people and many seem to particularly enjoy children. Due to their small size however, a Norwich Terrier, (especially a young puppy) may not be a good fit for a home with young children. All puppies test their limits

as they mature, and a young child could be hurt by sharp puppy teeth during the teething stages. Young children should never be left unattended with any dog.

The Bottom Line? Norwich Terriers are small dogs and are vulnerable in the hands of inexperienced, unsupervised, or heavy-handed children.

"How do you groom a wiry, double-coated dog?"
Norwich Terriers have a soft, downy undercoat for insulation, and a hard, wiry guard coat that helps keep them dry and dirt-free. Unless your dog rolls in something stinky, with daily brushing, a good diet, and regular "spot cleaning" your Norwich does not need bathing. The Norwich Terrier coat is as perfectly suited for going to ground, as it is for an outing on a cold or rainy day in the city or suburbs.

The process of grooming a wiry terrier coat is called "stripping." It is a skill you can learn with time and practice. The guard coat is pulled out by hand or by using a stripping knife. Pulling the dead coat out does not hurt the dog, and is necessary to achieve and maintain the hard, waterproof coat of the Norwich Terrier. Brushing is all that is necessary on a daily basis but weekly stripping sessions will help keep the coat tidy. A correct coat will shed minimally. If you learn the basics, it will suffice for a pet coat, as opposed to a show coat, but even keeping a pet coat tidy is time consuming. Having a terrier hand-stripped by a professional groomer can be expensive, and groomers who know how to properly strip a terrier, are scarce. Some groomers will want to take a shortcut and use clippers on your Norwich – do not allow it! * The limited use of scissors in sensitive areas (such as the tummy and rear end) should present no problems for the pet coat. If you use clippers on the guard coat, you will be essentially cutting it off, leaving the undercoat exposed and then your dog will definitely shed. There are some early photos of Nigel on the Norwich Tales website before I learned to strip him. By the time he was a year old he no longer looked like a Norwich Terrier. His coat was long, soft, harder to keep clean, and he shed a lot. I finally learned to strip his coat and I am glad I did. * In the case of an older dog, you may want to consider using a tool such as a Mars Coat King or even use clippers, due to the skin sensitivity of some older dogs.

The Bottom Line? Grooming a Norwich Terrier is time consuming and/or expensive. If you groom your dog yourself, you will need to invest in a variety of tools for grooming your Norwich.

"Besides coat care, what else is necessary on a regular basis to maintain a Norwich Terrier?"

Besides regular coat care, there are other things that you will need to do to maintain and keep a check on your dog's health. Brushing teeth daily, trimming nails on a regular basis, and "spot cleaning" are all part of regular maintenance for your dog. A high quality diet will be an important part of your dog's overall health as well. Your Norwich will require bedding and toys, replacement collars and leashes from time to time, updated identification, as well and other miscellaneous items.

Above, I mentioned the things that *you* will do to maintain your dog, but do not forget about veterinary care. Puppies will need to finish the series of core vaccines, begun by the breeder. Your dog will require annual tests such as heartworm testing, and he may need heartworm preventive as well as flea medication. Whether you decide to use pharmaceuticals or natural remedies, it can be expensive. Sometimes dogs get sick, and sometimes they do things that make them sick (Nigel's ingestion of a decomposing toad comes to mind here), and sometimes the illness means a trip to the vet and a medication to cure. Sometimes diagnostics and surgery are necessary. If your vacation plans do not include your dog, you will need to find a reliable friend, family member, pet sitter, or boarding facility to care for him in your absence. Boarding options range from the basic cage accommodation, to a comfortable room and bed at a pet resort.

The Bottom Line? Dogs require consistent care. Veterinary care is expensive, and a necessity for the entire life of your dog. You will need to consider boarding options and associated costs when you make plans that do not include your dog. All possible expenditures should be considered before bringing a dog into your home!

FOR BETTER FOR WORSE, FOR RICHER FOR POORER, IN SICKNESS AND IN HEALTH…

Bringing a dog into your life is a major commitment and should never be done without calm, clear thinking and planning. While some may balk at the original price of a purebred, rigorously health-tested Norwich Terrier, that price is minuscule compared to the amount of money it will cost to care for and maintain him for the rest of his life.

There may be times in your life when you have plenty and times when you have little. There may be times when you and your dog enjoy robust health, and there may be times of illness. There may be times when you want to go somewhere but you can't, because you have a dog at home who needs to be fed and let out to relieve himself. Having a dog can sometimes be like having a child who will never leave home. When you commit to dog ownership you are obligating yourself to provide for him for the rest of his life. In my opinion the reason that many dogs wind up in shelters is due to lack of preparation, lack of understanding, and lack of commitment by the person who once wanted the dog in the first place.

A puppy is fun and silly, and can sometimes be a little trying as he learns his place in your human world; the adolescent dog can be a little frustrating as he moves from adorable pup to boundary-testing adolescent. Looking forward to your faithful, loving, adult companion is what got you through those first two stages, and the golden years are nothing less than bittersweet. When finally, you are called upon to make the decision to end a life that you have spent years protecting, it will go against everything you think and feel. You will want to run from the responsibility and give it to someone else – anything to not make the decision. But you are obligated in love to find the strength to release your faithful friend, and end any suffering. This will break your heart in ways you never could have imagined. This too is part of your responsibility as a dog owner.

A dog is time consuming. A dog is expensive. A dog does not always allow you the freedom to come and go as you please. A dog comes in from the rain and shakes on your clean floor. A dog wants to walk or play when you want to rest. A dog gets sick in the middle of the night. A dog will roll in something stinky or dig a muddy hole just as you are preparing to leave for work or a special evening out. A dog will make you find patience and creativity you never knew you had. A dog will make you feel loved and needed. A dog will make you laugh and will make you cry.

Loving a dog will change you forever, maybe even leaving you a better person than you were before.

Chapter 3
Breeders – Responsible vs. Reprehensible

FINDING YOUR NORWICH TERRIER BREEDER

There are some truly fine breeders of Norwich Terriers. These are people who know the breed very well, and have great love and affection, as well as respect for it. Occasionally they have puppies or adult dogs available for placement, but they do not take orders and sell puppies to strangers (no questions asked) over the Internet. On the other hand, there are some unscrupulous types who knowingly breed dogs that have health problems and/or bad temperaments. They do not test their breeding dogs because it is an investment they are unwilling to make. There are some who are so deceptive, they breed Norwich Terriers with Cairn Terriers and sell these mixes as purebred Norwich Terriers to an unwitting public. Some, even more brazen, sell Cairn Terriers with a docked tail as a Norwich Terrier. See the "Getting More Specific" section in Chapter 1 for a partial breed standard including official Norwich Terrier colors. Note that solid black and brindle are not listed! As with everything in life, there are the good, the bad, and the down right ugly. In the following pages we will examine the various types of breeders you may encounter.

THE GOOD

These breeders are called "hobby breeders." Along with health testing their dogs before breeding, they study pedigrees to make sure that any breeding they do is a further asset to the breed. In their spare time, they take their dogs to conformation classes, attend health seminars, and often spend their weekends traveling to dog shows. Doing these things with their dogs is their hobby – they do not make a living off of them.

A good place to start looking for a responsibly bred Norwich Terrier is The Norwich Terrier Club of America (NTCA) at www.norwichterrierclub.org. Not only can you learn more about the breed from those who know it best, but you can get contact information for breeders who belong to the club. In belonging to the national breed club, these breeders choose to abide by a strict code of ethics. You can also attend AKC sanctioned conformation shows so you can meet breeders and their dogs. Before attending a show, see if you can set up some appointments to speak with several breeders at the show, after they have finished showing their dogs. Conscientious breeders are happy to answer your questions and help educate you on their breed. They will give you an honest assessment of the breed and help you to determine if the breed would be a good match for your home and lifestyle.

SOME HALLMARKS OF A GOOD BREEDER

- The breeder's number one goal is to improve and strengthen the breed. They breed to the conformation standard (form follows function), which includes correct temperament.
- The breeder rigorously health tests breeding dogs for eyes, hips, and patellas. Test results are posted on the Canine

Health Information Center (CHIC) website. See Resources section for link. Some breeders have begun having their dogs scoped for possible Upper Airway Syndrome (UAS) related problems before breeding them.

- The breeder's dogs are registered with the American Kennel Club (AKC), which maintains the registry for purebred dogs in the U.S. The AKC sanctions dog events and teaches responsible dog ownership. For our neighbors in Canada, the nationally recognized breed club is the Canadian Kennel Club (CKC). Other registries, called "Pet Registries" have been created by the commercial breeding industry for the commercial breeding industry.
- The breeder shows his or her dogs to their championship in conformation shows. A "finished dog" means that it meets the breed standard when judged against other Norwich Terriers. There are occasions when a dog is not shown but is bred because of its excellent health and temperament, but this is done only by knowledgeable, experienced breeders, who have a specific goal in mind.
- The breeder has potential homes planned for any puppies that may not be suitable to be included in their future breeding program.
- The breeder rigorously screens prospective homes for suitability of puppy placement, and places the best suitable dog with that family.
- The breeder invites a prospective owner to visit their home and see their dogs.
- The breeder offers a health guarantee.
- The breeder has a contract that includes a stipulation that the dog will be spayed or neutered at the appropriate, agreed upon time.

- Breeder includes a stipulation in the contract that if for any reason purchaser can no longer care for the dog, the dog is to be returned to the breeder. This indicates a lifelong commitment to any dog they have bred.
- Breeder will not place a puppy before 10 weeks of age, which is the absolute youngest age for puppy sale as described by the Code of Ethics by the national breed club.
- Breeder makes himself or herself available to answer questions.
- If the puppy is going to a show home, the breeder agrees to mentor the new owner.
- If any of the above practices are not being done by a breeder you are interviewing, interview other breeders.

Responsible breeders and responsible pet owners are not the cause of overcrowded shelters and unwanted dogs!

THE BAD

There is another type of breeder called a "backyard breeder." This is someone who has pet dogs they breed to produce puppies to sell as pets to make extra money. This type of breeder is often uneducated about the health of the dogs they breed. Sometimes they own one or both breeding dogs and breed them because they are "pretty" or "sweet." While this may sound harmless, it raises some important questions: What health or temperament problems do the individual dogs have that are being passed on to their offspring? Will those dogs in turn be bred, further passing on these problems to unsuspecting buyers? While the world is certainly not a perfect place, and even the most rigorously tested dogs can produce offspring with health problems, when breeders test, it lowers the odds, because informed decisions are made *before* breeding.

Back yard breeders sell their puppies through local pet stores, their personal websites, puppies-for-sale retail websites, magazine or newspaper ads, or by posting a sign on a street corner. While some do offer some sort of contract, many sell without a contract or a stipulation to spay or neuter, thus perpetuating the backyard breeder cycle. These kinds of indiscriminate breeding practices can lead to unwanted puppies that eventually wind up in shelters or worse. Due to public ignorance, backyard breeders can sometimes succeed in selling their puppies at, or nearly the same price as a dog that has been bred based on conformation, pedigree research, health, and temperament.

THE UGLY

A puppy mill is a facility where large quantities of dogs are bred. They are usually producers of many breeds of dogs, especially small breeds. Dogs are kept in very poor conditions, with no regard for their general welfare or the welfare of their offspring. Dogs are bred for one reason only – to produce puppies to sell for maximum profit. Lower overhead equals higher profits, so little is spent on shelter or other necessities. To say that conditions in puppy mills are dreadful is simply not saying enough.

Puppy mill dogs are kept in cages in the back yard, or in some kind of makeshift shelter, forced to endure all weather conditions. These breeding animals literally eat, sleep, and eliminate in a small cage for their entire life. Sometimes for the sake of saving space, the cages are stacked, and one animal relieves itself upon another. They cannot help it – they have no place else to go. Imagine the angst and the mental instability this creates for an animal that is by nature, a clean animal – not eliminating where it eats and sleeps. Illness can spread rapidly through a facility like this. Many of these caged dogs have damaged feet and legs from spending their lives standing on wire. Veterinary care will not be pursued for a damaged limb; you don't need limbs for breeding. Females are bred repeatedly until they are no longer viable.

Dogs who are unfortunate enough to live their lives in a puppy mill do not know what it is like to live a normal life. You may have even seen the occasional television expose´ on a raided puppy mill. You can hear the overwhelming sound of insane barking and see the filthy and pathetic animals either standing rigid with fear, or frantically running back and forth in their filthy cages. These dogs are completely un-socialized. During their lifetime, they never know the gentle, loving touch of a human hand unless by some miracle, it is the hand of someone who has finally come to the rescue.

It is widely known that several states seem to have a higher concentration of puppy mills compared to others. These states include Pennsylvania, Missouri, Ohio, and Oklahoma among others. According to the ASPCA, "Puppy mills began sprouting up after World War II. In response to widespread crop failures in the Midwest, the United States Department of Agriculture began promoting purebred puppies as a fool-proof 'cash' crop... chicken coops and rabbit hutches were repurposed for dogs, and the retail pet industry – pet stores, large and small, boomed with the increasing supply of puppies from the new 'mills.' Today Missouri is considered the largest puppy mill state in the country."[1]

Some operations are inspected by the USDA, but, unfortunately, this does not mean that conditions are good. In a report released in May, 2010 by the US Department of Agriculture, it states "AC's (Animal Care unit) enforcement process was ineffective against problematic dealers."[2]

The puppies born into a puppy mill spend their first few weeks in the insanity of the puppy mill, and then are removed from their mother at approximately six to eight weeks of age. They will then be sent to a broker who distributes them to pet stores. In the pet store they spend the next few weeks (or months) in *another* cage waiting to be purchased. Unfortunately this six to eight week timeframe falls during a critical time in a puppy's life – a time of necessary socialization with humans, as well as the beginning of the first fear period. But, then again, this is a really cute stage, and getting a puppy to market while he *is* still cute is paramount to getting him sold. Puppy mill puppies can have chronic health problems inherited from their chronically ill parents. They can arrive at the pet store with other unseen illnesses such as intestinal parasites, or respiratory infections contracted in the puppy mill. These illnesses, chronic or not, then become the emotional and financial burden for the buyer.

The emergence of the Internet has allowed puppy mills to sell their puppies to a much wider audience. In addition to retail stores, they, like the backyard breeder, can sell their puppies on any number of "puppies-for-sale" retail websites or through their own websites. They take your "order" and ship your puppy to you. This poses an interesting question: *If you order a puppy from a website, how do you know that the puppy you are choosing from a photo and description, is the puppy you are actually getting?* Simply put, you don't. Case in point, in late 2005 I discovered that one of Nigel's puppy photos had been stolen from the Norwich Tales website and was being used on a well-known puppies-for-sale website. They were even using his real name in the advertisement! Considering that Nigel was over seven *years* old at the time I discovered the stolen photo, I can assure you it was a scam. I wonder what the person who "ordered" my Nigel received?

You might ask yourself, *"Who in their right mind would buy a dog from a puppy mill?"* Many people do without even knowing it. If you have purchased a dog from a pet store – even a nice high-end store in the mall – the dog came from a back yard breeder or some other large scale breeding facility. If you have purchased a dog over the Internet with no questions asked of you, you have purchased from a puppy mill. Remember, no responsible breeder would allow his or her puppies to be sold in a retail outlet or anywhere, where the suitability of a potential home could not be determined.

IN CONCLUSION

When you buy from a puppy mill you may think you are rescuing a dog from a terrible fate, and on one hand you might be, but you are also becoming part of the economics of supply and demand. Buyers keep puppy mills in business. There is a good chance you could wind up with a dog that is riddled with problems ranging from behavioral to health issues. Your experience of dog ownership might turn out to be one of much frustration, grief, and financial woes. Even if you do wind up with a sweet, well balanced, and healthy dog that will give you pleasure for years to come, you helped the puppy mill cycle to continue, further enslaving the unfortunate dogs who remain there.

Researching breeders is different from finding the first breeder with an available puppy and ending your search there. The point of your research should be finding the *right* breeder, not just the first available puppy. If you suspect that the person you are working with is a back yard breeder or puppy mill on any scale, it would be wise for you to take a step back. If you rush in just to get a dog quickly, you could be very sorry you did.

Chapter 4
Welcome Home!

PREPARING FOR YOUR BUNDLE OF JOY

So you have done everything you were supposed to. You have thought seriously about bringing a dog into your home, and you understand the time and commitment a dog will require. You have thought realistically about the financial responsibilities, and you have found a breeder who meets your high standards. Now you are told that the breeder has a puppy available and they think your home would be the perfect fit for one of their furry little bundles of joy! Before you can bring your pup home however, you need to take care of some things that will make the transition safer and easier for everyone.

ESTABLISHING A HEALTH CARE PLAN

If you are new to having a pet and have not chosen a veterinarian, you should do so before you bring your puppy home. A good place to start is by asking trusted friends who have the same high standards that you do. Your veterinarian will provide among other services, finishing the necessary core (or "puppy") vaccines that your breeder started, and can provide regular checkups for your growing pup. He or she can also recommend and prescribe the appropriate medications for heartworm and fleas that are best suited to your region of the country. Since you never know when your pet will require a surgical procedure, having an experienced surgeon in your corner is essential. Your veterinarian can also make recommendations for a specialist if a need should arise. As the holistic approach becomes more accepted in western cultures, you may want to consider also seeking out the advice of a holistic vet for information and assistance with diet and nutrition, and alternative therapies and remedies if a particular health situation calls for it. In recent years some conventional veterinary practices have welcomed a holistic vet to their staff due to consumer demands.

Visit several veterinary offices in your area before making your decision. The following are some of the things I ask myself when looking for a veterinarian:

- Was a tour proudly offered by the staff?

- Is the office clean and organized?
- Are the exam rooms and surgical suites clean?
- Is the staff friendly and welcoming? Observe them with other clients and *their* pets. Is there a genuine concern for pet patients and their people?
- Is the waiting room packed and chaotic or is there order and calm?
- Is this practice convenient both in location and office hours?
- Do they offer any emergency services?
- How many veterinarians are on staff? What is their level of experience? Are there specialists on staff? Can you meet one of the veterinarians?
- How many technicians are on staff?
- What other services are offered, i.e., boarding, grooming, x-ray, or ultrasound testing?

After you have visited several offices in your area, choose the one you feel best meets your standards and expectations. Make an appointment in advance so that your vet can see your new pup within a day or two of his arrival home. See Resources section for websites with vet listings in your area.

Always remember, even if you have taken your dog to a particular vet for several visits, if something does not feel right, choose another vet for a second opinion or for a complete change in your dog's care. You are your dog's advocate and you know him better than anyone. If you do not feel heard or understood by a particular vet, choose another.

Another service to familiarize yourself with is the Emergency Vet clinic. These clinics provide emergency care after regular veterinary business hours. It is very important to know where these clinics are located; you do not want to be looking for the clinic in the middle of the night with a sick dog in your car! If there is more than one Emergency Vet clinic, or "E-vet" clinic in your area, it would be advantageous to visit them all to get a feel for what you like and do not like.

PUPPY PROOFING

Before you bring a puppy into your home, you will need to puppy proof it. Lie on the floor and you will be able to see your home from his unique perspective. Remove all small, forgotten objects from under furniture, because a puppy with a small object is as vulnerable as a baby with one. Move or remove things that you do not want him to investigate. If you have children, begin preparing them ahead of time to get into the habit of *not* leaving things on the floor. Of course this does not mean that you permanently remove the things that make your house a home and allow your pup to do as he pleases, but first you have to invest time in training him, and teaching him what is his to play with and what is not.

Be sure to caution your children and guests about your curious puppy and advise them to use the utmost care when handling certain foods, beverages, and other "off-limit" things around him. Here are several reasons why:

- Puppies have delicate systems and suddenly adding new foods to his diet can cause vomiting, gas, and diarrhea. A small, young puppy can dehydrate very quickly with a bad case of diarrhea.

- Besides having delicate tummies, puppies have good memories. If you do not want your pup to beg every time you eat, do not feed him while you are eating.
- Some human foods are dangerous to dogs. Foods including (but not limited to) grapes, raisins, caffeine, cooked bones, and onions, can be harmful to dogs. Xylitol, an ingredient in sugar free gum and candy, and other human products is very toxic to dogs. Ingestion of just one or two pieces of sugarless gum for example, can result in the death of a small dog.
- Alcoholic beverages and tobacco are absolutely forbidden.
- Use caution when handling human medications. A dropped tablet can quickly be snatched up by a dog.
- Household cleansers, pest control, and automobile products such as antifreeze, are highly toxic to dogs if ingested, and can cause organ failure and even death.
- Obtain a poisonous plants list specific for your geographical area.

The best course of action is to keep your pup under your watchful eye, using a crate or an exercise pen (X-pen) to keep him safe and out of mischief when you are unable to watch him.

Now that your house is ready, let's look at your yard. Is your fence suitable for keeping a small pup in? If escape is possible you may need to put up some temporary wire to keep him from slipping out. Are there gaps under the fence? Remember, Norwich Terriers are expert diggers! Some breeders recommend that you bury your fence at least one foot, to assure that your Norwich cannot burrow out. Do you have a pool? If so, you need to make sure that your dog – puppy or adult – is under your supervision at all times.

I have included a Puppy Needs list at the end of this book, which will be of help to get you started with some basic supplies for your puppy.

IT'S TIME!

Before picking up your puppy, you will have had many discussions with your breeder, including what he or she will provide for you. Most will offer a blanket or towel with familiar scents, your puppy's favorite toy, and in some instances, a small supply of water. Some will additionally offer a starter collar and leash set. You will want to bring a crate (or airline approved travel bag if flying), his identification, and perhaps a new toy for maximum interest. When you pick up your pup, the breeder will review the contract with you, give you the vaccine schedule, and will review and give you your AKC registration papers.

ALLOW ME TO INTRODUCE MYSELF

I have talked a lot about bringing home a puppy but there is another kind of new family member we have yet to discuss: the adult Norwich Terrier. The adult dog is a special placement for a breeder. Sometimes he or she may have a young adult, that they were hoping would work out in the conformation ring, but for some reason it didn't. Or, a breeder may have a lovely finished champion who has had a couple of litters to continue the lines of the kennel, but now needs to place this dog to make it possible to continue working with the next generation. These placements are bittersweet because it is likely that the breeder has been involved in every stage of this dog's life. Adult Norwich Terriers are every bit as lovable and are as quick to bond to you as is a puppy – without all the work of housebreaking and the pain of teething! My girl Divot was placed with us at the age of three, and there was absolutely no issue with bonding. Her arrival and integration into our home was, in many ways, easier than was puppy Nigel's.

If you are bringing home an adult Norwich, be sure to show him or her what is and is not acceptable right away. For example if he immediately makes himself at home on your sofa and this was not something you planned on, you must teach him that the sofa is not his bed, then show him his own comfortable place. If you allow something for a while and change your mind later it will be confusing for him. Boundaries shown in a clear, gentle, and consistent manner will make for a smooth transition for any adult dog.

If you are bringing home an adult Norwich and you already have another adult dog, but have not had the opportunity to introduce them, if possible introduce them on neutral territory. Once home, allow the new pack-mates to explore together under your supervision. Be sure each has a place to retreat to if they need some space. The two of them will work out their place in the pack and this will most likely be very subtle.

A FEW THOUGHTS ABOUT PACKS AND COMMUNICATION

If you are an experienced dog owner, integrating a puppy or an adult dog into your home probably comes very natural to you, but if you are bringing home your first puppy or dog, you may have some misconceptions about living with a dog. Many naively think that showering your dog with love and affection, feeding him, and playing whenever he wants to, makes for the perfect family member. Not that these activities aren't a fun part of having a dog but those things come after meeting his need for structure. Dogs are pack animals. A pack is a structured social group in which there is a hierarchy or ranking system. In the wild, the "top dogs" or pack leaders, are usually the parents of many of the pack members, and their pack looks to them for providing among other things, direction and security. Even young puppies instinctually understand the hierarchy, and display dominant and submissive behaviors at play and when interacting with the rest of the pack.

Establishing yourself as your dog's leader does not mean that you rule with an iron fist, instilling fear by your very presence. Being your dog's leader means you are confident, consistent, and give clear direction of what you want and do not want, and you provide for his needs – both physical and psychological.

A respected Norwich Terrier breeder and friend of mine concurs, and says that having the opportunity to observe mothers and pups is the best education one can get on how to understand dogs. She told me a fascinating story about the matriarch of her pack, raising her first puppy. She said, "This happened when the puppy was about four weeks old. Suddenly I heard him crying and screaming. I came into the room where they were, and she was holding him down. When he tried to get up, she pushed him back down and held him there. She cleaned his face, ears, and genitals thoroughly and she did not let him up, until he stopped fighting and submitted to her. When he stopped fighting, she let him up. Another time I watched as she offered him a toy and then she took it back. Then she gave the toy back, and then took it back from him. She did this several times and I think she was instilling in him, *'This is mine but I'm letting you play with it. When I want it back, you will surrender it to me.'* She was reinforcing her role as the dominant dog and he accepted it. I'm not sure what caused her to be so strict with him but apparently she saw that he needed to be brought down a peg occasionally, and she was going to be the one to do it! She has been a remarkable teacher to her pups and to me."

That puppy, (now 11 years old at the time of this writing) is a beautiful finished champion, a Westminster Kennel Club Best of Breed winner, and the sire to another generation of healthy, Norwich Terriers with excellent temperaments – and he still lives at home with his mother!

Take a lesson from nature, and try to lead with the clarity and confidence of a mother dog, with the goal being a puppy who understands his place as a follower, secure in your leadership. If you do so, you will be relating to your dog in the way *he* understands. While dogs can and do learn sizable vocabularies, spoken communication is not their natural means of communication. They use body language – from nose to tail and everything in between. Remember, English is their *second* language!

DOG WILLING

As a responsible adult, you probably carry a variety of insurance coverage and you most likely have a will, trust, or other legal directive. No one likes to think about their demise, but knowing what will happen to your family members if you are no longer able to take care of them is reassuring. But, what about your dog? Your Norwich Terrier is also a member of your family and is possibly the most vulnerable in an emergency, as other people may view him as "just a dog." Please be sure to give thought to and discuss with your family members or trusted circle of friends, who among them would be ready and willing to take your dog in the event of your death, or sudden inability to care for him. Put this directive in your will or trust, and let your breeder know who you have appointed so that he or she may offer assistance in helping get the dog acclimated if necessary. If you do not have anyone in your family or circle of friends who is willing or able to care for your dog in your absence, be sure to discuss this with your breeder and make a clear directive in your legal documents that your dog is to be returned to his breeder. Talk to your attorney about the options available to protect your pet.

A little preparation means that your beloved pet will not wind up in a shelter or worse.

Part II - Chapter 5

A Norwich For Dummies

HEAD KNOWLEDGE VERSUS PRACTICAL EXPERIENCE

If you have gotten this far you might be thinking that I have been able to share some wisdom or helpful guidance because I am one of those people who naturally "understands" dogs.

You may have even learned a few things, which would please me greatly, but in all honestly many of the valuable things I have learned were the result of doing it wrong the first time. My mother always said, *"Some people just like to learn the hard way."* When she said that, I was *sure* she wasn't talking about me.

AND THE WINNER IS…

"May I have…the Norwich Terrier!"

"I won! Honey, my dog won! Willum won!" I yelled excitedly, clapping my hands as the Norwich Terrier, Ch. Chidley Willum the Conquerer[1] was named Best in Show at the prestigious Westminster Kennel Club Dog Show. Actually, it was not *my* dog that won – I had never even met Willum. In fact, I had never met *any* Norwich Terrier before.

It was February 15, 1994, and Mike and I were watching the popular televised dog show on a cold, snowy evening in Michigan. I was really taken with the handsome little black and tan Willum when he first strutted out in the Terrier Group. Considering what I knew about conformation shows (nothing), I thought he should win because he was the cutest dog there so I picked him as "my dog." That is certainly not the way the winner of a conformation show is determined but what did I know?

We had been discussing getting a dog and we thought there was no better way to start our research than by watching this famous dog show, with its wide variety of breeds in attendance. As we watched each individual dog being presented, we discussed our wants, likes and dislikes based on size, description of temperament, physical needs, grooming requirements, and what we were generally attracted to. We knew that we wanted a breed that was small and portable, but sturdy, not dainty. We were interested in a dog that was active but not hyper. We hoped to find a breed with a coat that did not require professional grooming. We were concerned about getting a breed that might be prone to excessive barking since Mike was working from home. We both agreed that the Norwich Terrier had many of the traits we were looking for. One roadblock to dog ownership was that we lived in a condo at the time and we could not even have a dog. So, we tucked the dream of our little dog into our hearts, started doing our research, and worked toward buying a house with a yard so we could make a proper home for our little pup. It would be another four years before we would meet our little Nigel, a descendent of the handsome Willum.

THE WORK BEGINS

At the time we began our research on the Norwich Terrier in 1994, the Internet was a relatively new resource, and the pace of gathering information could be excruciatingly slow, so we went to bookstores looking for any information on the Norwich Terrier breed, and I called our local kennel club for additional resources. Considered a rare breed, information on the Norwich Terrier in particular, was scarce to say the least. As time went by we continued to scour bookstores and the Internet, and began attending dog shows so we could see and meet Norwich Terriers. We met a couple of breeders who worked together, co-owning several dogs, and we felt comfortable with them so we began to communicate with them on a regular basis. We asked all the questions we could think of about the breed, and they patiently answered them, and in turn, asked us questions about ourselves and our lifestyle. We visited their homes a few times, and were thrilled to spend time with their dogs. We stayed in contact, and asked to be put on their waiting list for a puppy for sometime in the future.

In June of 1998, we finally bought our dream home, a home in which we could raise our dream dog. I e-mailed one of the breeders and told her that we had bought a new home and would be moving in shortly after returning from a two-week trip. I gave her our new contact information and said that we were ready for a puppy when she was! Three days after moving into our brand new home, I received an e-mail informing me, *"We have a puppy for you!"* I was ecstatic!

Mike and I are nothing if not organized, and by day three, we were completely unpacked, with the house mostly in order. I ran to the garage where Mike was setting up his tool bench and I shared this exciting news with him. His response certainly was not what I expected. He said, "Honey, we just moved in to a brand new house three days ago. We should wait a while, you know, get more settled first. Maybe wait a year." He went back to organizing his tools as if dismissing the idea. If he had said, *"And by the way, I'm leaving you,"* I probably would have felt less pain than I did at that moment. I was crushed. My dream was shattered! I, a mature adult woman was reduced to the tears and sentiments of a five year old as I sunk down on the step, head in hands crying, "But we've gotta have a puppy!"

I'm not proud of it. That has never been my way of handling disagreements in my marriage, but, *my* puppy was just three hours away (that is a mere 170 miles) from my loving arms and this man was telling me to wait a *year*? The thought of someone else raising *my* puppy was....well, it was unthinkable! Two days later Mike looked wistfully at the brand new living room carpet, and we were on our way across the state to get our puppy.

It was four years and four months after we saw Willum win Best in Show at the Westminster Kennel Club Dog Show that we brought our little Norwich Terrier, "Nigel" home. He was cute, and silly, and he was feisty! We had spent four years researching, reading, meeting breeders, and even meeting a few Norwich Terriers along the way preparing for this very moment! And as it turns out, we were utterly *unprepared…*

A NORWICH FOR DUMMIES

We *thought* we had done everything right. Researched the breed? Yes. Asked ourselves the hard questions about dog ownership and lifelong commitment? Yes. Found knowledgeable breeders? Yes. Found a good vet? Yes. Read books on training? Yes. Bought everything on the "puppy needs" list? Yes.

The day came to pick up Nigel. We loaded his new crate and some toys into the back of the SUV and off we went. We spent some time getting to know Nigel and his siblings, chatting with the breeders, asking some last minute questions, and reviewing paperwork. We took a few photos, there were hugs all around, and we were off – ready to start our new life with our puppy! The trip was approximately three hours so we decided to stop for a break about half way, and see if Nigel needed to relieve himself. We walked him around a bit but he did not seem to have to go, so we put him in the back of the vehicle on the folded down seats and stood there admiring him. We let him explore a little and play with his new toys. As we were marveling about how adorable he was, we didn't notice the curious way he was sniffing and circling. We had wanted him to relieve himself and he did, just not when or where we wanted him to. Okay, *that* was a mistake we won't repeat. The rest of the trip went smoothly. When we got home, we excitedly showed Nigel around his new home. The mistake that-was-not-to-be repeated, actually *was* repeated shortly after our arrival home, this time on the new living room carpet. Perhaps it was time to reexamine that information on housebreaking...

Though we were filled with book knowledge, we had absolutely no practical, instinctual experience about how to live with a dog, let alone a puppy.

THE HEARTBREAK OF HOUSEBREAK

Housebreaking does not have to be a difficult hurdle to get over because our dogs come equipped with something amazing to help in this process – instinct! Housebreaking does not need to be a stressful time for either of you – that is unless you are a dog in the hands of two dummies who know very little about those amazing instincts you came with, or about how to properly teach you what they want you to do.

Our dream house was perfect. Perfect for us that is. It was *not* perfect for a small puppy. Our elegant two-story home had flights of stairs *everywhere.* In order for Nigel to go outside to go potty, I would have to carry him down any number of staircases. He was too young and too small to navigate any steps. The first plan, and the one that seemed to make the most sense for the long run, was to take him down a flight of stairs, through the walkout basement and out to the fenced back yard. We would need to carry Nigel up and down until he could do it himself. Making this exit choice a little challenging however, was a solid door that led down those steps – a door which gave no indication to a puppy that it lead "outside" or anywhere for that matter. I figured that in time, Nigel would learn that this was the door that I carried him to, and eventually he would go there and ask to be let out. Unfortunately, over the months that we worked on this plan, Nigel did not seem to distinguish this door from anything else in the house and never went near the door on his own. Scrapping the first plan, we moved on to the second plan.

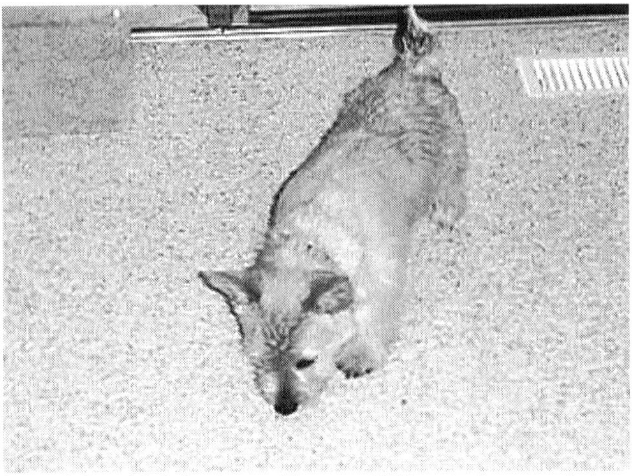

We learned that this behavior could mean, "Where is that treat I dropped?" Or it could mean, "I'm going to pee here." Mostly, it meant the latter...

This new plan involved using an exit to the back yard by way of the deck. We hoped that Nigel would see "outside" through the large patio door, and make the association with needing to relieve himself, then I would carry him down the deck steps until he was big enough to do it himself. Living in a tree house-like setting was beautiful, but not at all practical for house-breaking a small puppy. After a few weeks of trying *this*, we realized that soon enough, winter would set in and Michigan winters are not conducive to walking up and down 13 snow covered steps countless times a day with a puppy tucked under your arm. This was not a short *or* long-term solution. So, we abandoned *that* idea.

The third plan involved putting some newspapers on the deck to at least give him a starter place to go. Thinking this might be helpful to get his mind and body moving in the right direction, he could at least walk to the big patio door, see "outside," make all the mental connections and then viola! We would have ourselves a trained dog in no time. After this was accomplished, we would just need to reintroduce him to the door leading to the basement when he was big enough to manage the steps. Nigel did manage to eliminate a time or two on those papers but after some consideration, Mike changed his mind and decided that he really did not want Nigel relieving himself on the deck – papers or not. I was frustrated because I knew that continually changing the plan was confusing to Nigel and trying to accommodate Mike's ever changing ideas and wishes, was increasing my frustration. Getting new carpet suddenly seemed like a less expensive option than losing my sanity.

Nigel was a smart pup, and I knew that he would catch on if we were consistent and he was allowed to go through the whole process from start to finish, but a small puppy could not execute any of the plans we tried. A few more months went by and it was hit and miss – mostly us missing his signals, and me hitting my head against the wall because I could not get my puppy housebroken.

After some discussions with those more experienced than me, I made a new plan. If you are keeping track, this is the fourth plan. (Is it any wonder this poor puppy was confused?) My new plan was to take Nigel out the *front* door. This door was never included in any previous discussions because it was a forbidden door. It was forbidden because it led to the front lawn, which was sheer perfection. Though the front yard was not fenced in, the front door had the easiest access to outside. The front porch had only *one* step down to the sidewalk and the grass – at nearly nine months old, Nigel could do *that*! This plan would allow Nigel the opportunity to walk out the door on his own four feet to do his business, so I was confident that it would click for him if only allowed to try. Now would be a good time to point out that Mike is a lawn fanatic. His beautiful lawn would make any greens keeper proud to call his own and even a little envious. Suffice it to say, when I told him about my new plan he was not on board with this idea of Nigel going potty in the *front* yard.

I ignored Mike's pleas of "Honey please – no!" I attached Nigel's leash saying, "Let's go outside and go potty!" I took him out the front door, and walked him to the area by the mailbox where all the good stuff happens. He sniffed all the interesting smells, squatted and relieved himself. After he went, I praised him like he had just come home with a record breaking SAT score. His freedom secured for a few hours, we played and then he napped. The moment he woke up I said, "Let's go outside and go potty" and I walked toward the front door, leash in hand, with him happily following me like we had been doing this for years. By late the next day he was going to the front door on his own as if to say, "I have to go!" And that was it. In the span of one day, after trying a series of complicated, silly ideas, the best idea was right in front of us – all we had to do was open our eyes, open the front door, and eventually open a bag of lawn patch seed. The most important thing was that Nigel was making all the right connections and he was on his way to being trained! The next thing I added was to teach him to bark once when we went to the door. Once he was reliable doing that, (by now he was bigger and more coordinated), I took him to the door that lead to the basement and thus the backyard and said, "Lets go outside and go potty!" Soon he was going to *that* door, barking once, and out we went to his fenced yard. It's truly a wonder he didn't just pack up and leave us...

~ Teachable Moment ~
Housebreaking does not have to be heartbreaking!

As I have already mentioned, your dog comes with an amazing instinct that, if understood, can help make housebreaking a smooth transition and a less stressful time for everyone. A dog's natural instinct is to be clean – they do not like to eliminate where they eat and sleep. When pups are young and still suckling, their mother "cleans up" the den or in our dogs' case, the whelping box. In the wild, a clean den would make pups less conspicuous to predators, and this behavior has carried over to our domestic dogs. Once the pups start eating solid food, mom stops cleaning up after them, but by this time it is ingrained in them to be clean where they eat and sleep. When our pups come to us, it is important that we understand the instinct to be clean and continue using it to our advantage. You can make it easy for your pup to succeed by first understanding his instincts, and then correctly using the tools you have at your disposal.

The Crate
The crate is a wonderful tool. There are a variety of crate options for the pet owner: the versatile plastic crate with a handle, wire crates, or for those who want a crate that makes a statement, there are some higher priced models that come in wood or rattan. Though definitely the most attractive, I would caution against a pricey wood or rattan model until your puppy matures and won't chew on it. Wire allows more air to circulate so if you live in a hot climate this would be a good choice for you. Which ever type you choose, make sure that your puppy has *only* a positive experience with it. If you are working with a

responsible breeder, your pup will already have positive crate experience. If he shows hesitation about his new crate, help him move beyond it by placing his familiar scent blanket or towel inside. Also, place tiny treats in the crate for him to find. At first, do not close the door when he goes in. Allow him to relax and explore it with the door open so that he does not think that entering the crate automatically means confinement. You can begin closing the door, as he gets more comfortable with it. Feeding your puppy in his crate will also create a very positive association with it, as well as reinforce the instinct to not soil where he eats and sleeps. Anything to do with the crate must be positive! Make sure that your pup understands that only really good things happen in the crate. Never place your dog in his crate as punishment!

The X-Pen (exercise pen)

In addition to the crate, our breeder had recommended that we get an X-pen, (portable exercise pen) for Nigel. This not only protected our home but, allowed him a safe place to play or sleep when I could not watch him, without confining him to his crate. The purpose of the X-pen is to create a "living area" for your pup. Think of it as giving your puppy his own room. The area you create should be on a hard surface that is easy to clean, but make sure there is soft bedding available in the space too. If possible, locate the X-pen near the exit door your pup will use to go outside. This will make getting him from his clean place to outside easier, with fewer chances for mistakes as training progresses. Place his crate, toys, and water bowl in his living area. This will allow your pup to have a little more freedom than being confined to his crate, while keeping him and your home safe when you aren't watching him.

Nigel "does time" in his X-pen.

A special place, a special word, and a schedule

- Establish a potty spot for your pup. Dogs are creatures of habit. The scent stimulus will help him to know what he is supposed to do when you take him to his spot.

- Establish a word or phrase to use when you want him to eliminate. The word will eventually become associated with the action of eliminating.

- At first you will need to carry your young puppy outside so that he does not "go" on your way to the door. Eventually he can follow you.

Following is an example of a potty schedule you can use to get started. Your schedule will dictate the times you will use but you will get the general idea.

Puppy's First Potty Schedule (example)	
6:00 a.m.	Take puppy to potty spot to urinate.
6:15 a.m.	Feed puppy in crate.
6:30 a.m.	Take puppy to potty spot for bowel movement.
9:30 - 10:00 a.m.	Take puppy to potty spot to urinate. If he goes, he earns supervised freedom. If not, back in crate for 15 more minutes. Repeat until he goes.
Noon	Feed lunch in crate.
12:30 p.m.	Take puppy to potty spot for bowel movement and urination. If he goes, he earns supervised freedom. If not, back in crate for 15 more minutes. Repeat until he goes.
3:00 - 3:30 p.m.	Take puppy to potty spot to urinate. If he goes, he earns supervised freedom. If not, back in crate for 15 more minutes. Repeat until he goes.
6:00 p.m.	Feed dinner in crate.
6:15 p.m.	Take puppy to potty spot for bowel movement and urination. If he goes, he earns supervised freedom. If not, back in crate for 15 more minutes. Repeat until he goes.
7:00 - 7:30 p.m.	Pick up water for the evening.
10:00 - 10:30 p.m.	Take puppy to potty spot to urinate. Then crate for the night.

First thing in the morning, take your puppy out to his potty spot and say the special word/command. Repeat word or phrase *calmly* as he is going. A calm repetition of the word or phrase will create an association between the word(s) and his actions without distracting him. When he has finished, praise him. Then he earns supervised freedom. When the time is approaching for him to need go again, take him out (time between outings will depend on his age). If he goes, he earns supervised freedom. If he does not go, place him in his crate for approximately 15 minutes, then take him outside again. Continue to apply the 15-minute rule until he does go. Repeat this process throughout the day. Young puppies especially, need to empty their bladder after waking from a nap, after play, or after eating. Be sure to take up his water bowl several hours before bedtime to avoid putting him to bed with a full bladder. The general rule is that puppies up to four months old usually need to urinate approximately every three to four hours, and most can go up to six hours overnight. This means that for a while at least, you'll have to take him out in the middle of the night so that he can relive himself.

Puppies usually have bowel movements after each meal, so feed your pup in his crate. Close the door while he is eating. Give him about 15 minutes to eat in his crate and then take him out to potty. If he eliminates, praise him and give him supervised freedom. If he does not go, place him back in the crate, wait 10-15 minutes and try again. Getting him to calmly walk around can help produce a bowel movement. After he goes, he earns supervised freedom. Puppies have short digestive tracts. Remember, when something goes in, something will soon need to come out.

As your puppy ages, the time between outings will increase, and you will be able to expand his living area. He can be placed in his X-pen area rather than his crate between potty outings or when you cannot watch him. Just as he did with his crate, as he takes ownership of his X-pen area, his instincts will be to keep *it* clean because that is where he eats and sleeps. Do not wait until he is six or nine months old to introduce him to other parts of your home. Let him explore other rooms of your house with you, after he has eliminated, so that these rooms will also be considered part of his living area. Eventually he will grow beyond the need to be confined. At first it may help to create a chart to note the times of the day that your puppy eliminates, especially if there is more than one family member taking him out.

Mistakes *will* happen – this is a process and a milestone in your puppy's life. Be patient, be proactive, and never punish your pup for a mistake. Never allow yourself to think that your puppy (or your adult dog for that matter) is soiling your house out of spite. Dogs do not possess such emotions.

Where did we go wrong?

I had a crate and an X-pen for Nigel so why were my initial attempts to housebreak him unsuccessful? In a word: inconsistency. We did not create a schedule for Nigel, and sometimes we felt bad for confining him to his X-pen, so we took him out to play with him without having him earn supervised freedom. Also, we had not created a special potty spot for him. As you may recall, we changed his potty spot several times so he was confused by all the changes. Once I did create that potty spot (the mailbox) and became consistent with my behavior, he caught on quickly. Looking back with hindsight, most puppies are raised to relieve their full bladders on papers, shavings, or rags, so another porous surface, such as carpet, is the main association in their mind. *We* certainly didn't make that association! When you begin the housebreaking process, you must change that association specifically to "outdoors."

~ Teachable Moment ~
Submissive or Excited Urination.

Since we are on the topic of eliminations, now might be a good time to discuss a problem that more than just a few owners of puppies and young dogs struggle with: excited urination or submissive urination. Because both excited and submissive urination could have a physical component involved, have your pup examined by your veterinarian to rule out a physical problem. If it is strictly a behavioral problem, both conditions can be overcome with time, understanding, and patience.

Excited Urination

Excited urination happens when your dog is at a heightened level of excitement. As a puppy, Nigel was an excited urinator. Here are a few things that I learned to help him overcome the problem.

- Identify what makes your puppy excitedly urinate.
- If your puppy excitedly urinates when you come home, you will need to change the way you greet him. Ignore him until he is calm. Do not speak to him and do not make eye contact. Take him out to empty his bladder immediately.
- Once he is calm – still without making eye contact – calmly get down to his level to allow him to be near you. You may pet him but if he gets too excited, then stop. You can work toward that later.
- Do not speak during this time. Too much verbal dialog can cause him to get excited again.

- Before guests arrive, be proactive and make sure he has emptied his bladder.
- One of the most difficult things to overcome will be training your dog-loving guests not to excite your puppy. Many people will have a hard time ignoring a cute puppy and may be resistant to comply with your instruction to ignore him. This will undoubtedly make modifying this behavior much more difficult. Your guests should follow the same protocol you do: ignore him until he is calm, do not make eye contact, and do not speak to him in excited tones.
- It should go without saying, never yell at or punish your pup for excited urination. It certainly will not help. Your consistency in training, time, and your puppy's maturity will be key in overcoming this issue.

Submissive Urination

Submissive urination is when your dog urinates "inappropriately" out of submission. I use the word inappropriately in quotes because in the natural world of dogs, submissive urination is not inappropriate, but on your floor or your feet, it seems very inappropriate. Some of the body language characteristics of a submissive dog are: ears folded back, head lowered, tail tucked, crawling on his belly, or rolling on his back, belly exposed. NOTE: Submission does not necessarily signal *fear*. Submission to a higher-ranking pack member is natural to dogs, but a submissive dog as well as one that is truly fearful may submissively urinate.

Not having experience with a submissive urinator, but having studied the problem somewhat, I learned that the reconditioning approach seems very much the same as with an excited urinator.

- Identify what makes your puppy submissively urinate.
- Once you have identified the triggers, learn to ignore him during those times. When he tries to submit to you, walk away without making eye contact. Do not speak to him.
- When your pup is calm – still without making eye contact – pet or scratch his chin, chest or tummy, rather than his head. Many people naturally want to pet a dog's head, and while some dogs may enjoy it, some dogs, especially the submissive ones, may feel threatened by a hand coming down upon them.
- Participate in activities that may build his confidence as well as your bond. Work through some training exercises always ending with a successfully completed one, join an agility or obedience class, go for walks together and praise him for good walking manners, or participate in any other activity he enjoys.
- As with an excited urinator, do not yell at or punish your dog for submissive urinating. It will certainly not help and will most definitely make the problem worse! If you are not able to make progress with this issue, consult with your vet or a canine behaviorist.

A NORWICH TALE

Lift a Leg – Any Leg! – September 1998

A novice leg lifter makes for a humorous tale.

When Nigel was about five months old, he began to act like he knew instinctively that he was supposed to be doing "something" when he went potty. Sometimes he would squat like puppies do, but then try to lift a leg while squatting, which was difficult and awkward looking, but certainly fun to watch. As time went on, the behavior became more pronounced and then it seemed to click that he should lift his leg and aim high.

Sometimes un-level surfaces could cause this novice to lose his balance when lifting his leg, but he was determined to lift just the same. One day as we were leaving our yard for a walk, Nigel stopped by our mailbox to see who might have already been by. We called this "checking his P-mail." He sidled up to the mailbox and started to squat and then it was as if it suddenly occurred to him, *"I forgot to lift my leg!"* Being the novice that he was however, he lifted a *front* leg and then as if realizing the mistake, he then lifted a back leg! I could not help but laugh at him, thinking that he looked more like chameleon on the hot desert sand than a puppy. As I laughed at him, he innocently looked up as if to say, *"And what's so funny?"* ^..^

A NORWICH TALE

Waving the White Flag – December 1998

But surrender is not actually an option!

Nigel, like all puppies, is interested in little else but having fun. Unfortunately, sometimes the things he thinks are fun can be inconvenient for me to say the least. I am speaking of his habit of what I call "waving the white flag." Just last week, I thought Nigel was in the room with me but apparently he had slipped away. I called his name and I became a little worried when I could not find him. Just as I was heading upstairs, I saw a small reddish blur followed by a long white kite-like tail, streaking across the landing, going from the guest bathroom to the bedroom across the hall. Nigel had discovered the toilet paper in there! Admittedly, it was a rather funny sight, and he thought that my unsuccessful attempt to try to take away the toilet paper was equally amusing.

Additionally, it never fails that if a sock has been forgotten on the floor, Nigel will find it and before long, the chase is on. It is his rule of thumb to find the forgotten sock just as we are preparing to leave the house. Chasing a small dog with perceived "treasure" means that he only runs faster than you ever thought he could. Getting tough and demanding that he drop the sock does nothing, as he is sure I am kidding anyway. Working together like two predators to trap prey is the only way Mike and I can get a stolen sock back quickly.

The other game Nigel has created is the always crowd pleasing, *Steal the Napkin From the Guest's Lap*. This is by far his favorite game as it involves more interesting people than just Mike and me. What began as what we thought was a one-time breach of etiquette, has become Nigel's favorite game as he steals the napkin from a guest's lap and runs wild through the house with it. Fortunately our dinners are not formal and our friends are dog-loving people. My temporary solution has been to advise all guests to keep their napkin on the table. Any napkin properly placed on a lap that is stolen is now the guest's responsibility to retrieve! ^..^

Chapter 6
Growing Up and Growing Wiser

THE FORMATIVE YEARS

Nigel was adored by us before we even knew him – when he was still just a wish. When we brought him into our lives, he received an abundance of love and attention, but little in the way of meaningful discipline and direction, and it did not take long for him to become an overindulged, pushy, adolescent brat. Shortly after we brought him home, I checked out the only puppy class offered in our area. The class was all the way across town but I thought it was important so I checked into it anyway, but as I sat observing the class, I kept getting bitten by fleas! I opted not to return and thought that if we needed help I would go the private route rather than risk having my puppy infested with fleas.

We lived in western Michigan, which, at that time, had not fully embraced the "dog friendly" culture that many other parts of the country had, so there were not many dog friendly places to take Nigel to socialize. Much of his socialization opportunities outside of our home, revolved around neighborhood walks. Unfortunately, with only a few exceptions, much of his social interaction with other *dogs* was with overexcited, out of control dogs who were either pulling their owners like sidewalk skiers, or were lunging at us, excited to meet or something worse. There were two large parks nearby and we enjoyed taking Nigel there but inevitably someone would let their dog off leash in the park, and when the dog charged up to us running at full speed, little Nigel would go flat on the ground or try to get away. Nigel absolutely *loved* people but to him, most other dogs were a nuisance and they were of no value to him. Admittedly, looking back we knew nothing about how to live with and properly teach *our* dog, but then again if memory serves, there seemed to be an epidemic of that all around us.

By six months of age, besides lifting his leg, Nigel began to show other signs of "maturity." That is a polite way of saying that he began to hump everything he could – pillows, my arm, his toys –whatever vulnerable object he could grab on to was going to get humped. This was all starting to drive me a little crazy, but I considered it to be part of the maturation process. What I did not consider was that this was in part, also a display of dominance. He was beginning to test limits as all puppies will do. I must admit that I was a bit relieved when I dropped him off at the vet to be neutered. A few hours later the vet called to tell me that he had done well, was resting, and I could pick him up later. When we picked him up, he was still a little dopey, and as I squatted down to greet him he wobbled right past me to Mike. Like anyone else who knows nothing about dogs, I humanized him and I felt certain that he was blaming *me* for this. I felt terrible and cried all the way home. He was a little wobbly for the rest of the evening but by the next day, he seemed to be feeling much better.

This began Nigel's life long fear of the vet. It was probably partly founded on a natural dislike of going to a place where you are poked, prodded, and manipulated by strangers, but this fear was additionally, and unintentionally, fueled by me over time. During all of my research and gathering of knowledge about getting a dog, some important information I failed to grasp was how to *be* with your dog, and equally as important, how *not* to be with your dog. As a human being, and operating from the only perspective I have (which happens to be the human one), I wanted to comfort my frightened puppy. At the vet's office, when he began to whimper, I held and petted him, speaking as soothingly as a mother would to a weeping toddler who presents her with a scraped knee, "There, there Nigel. It's okay baby. You're such a good boy. Such a goooood booyyyyyy." All of my attempts to soothe never helped him move beyond his fear, but that did not stop me from continuing to use that approach. It was not working to allay his fears and unbeknownst to me it was instead reinforcing them.

~ Teachable Moment ~
There is a right time and a wrong time to praise!

Simply put: Do not praise your dog for being fearful. My words and actions toward frightened Nigel were to him, acceptance, praise and positive reinforcement for his fear. It should go without saying, do not praise *any* bad or unwanted behavior your dog displays. While this sounds like common sense, praising or approving of bad behavior happens frequently. You will see it if you observe enough people interacting with their dogs. For example I have witnessed countless people walking their dog and when the dog lunges at someone, rather than correcting the dog, the owner instead, attempts to calm the dog by petting him while saying something like, "It's okay Duke. It's okay. Good boy Duke, you're a good boy." They seem to think that if they affirm *to the dog* that he truly is a good dog, that he will suddenly stop the unwanted behavior, because after all, he is a good dog and he knows it. What they are doing is the opposite of what they intend to do – they are praising the dog and approving, even *encouraging* – the bad, or unwanted behavior by rewarding the dog with their soothing words and touch. Like the people who unwittingly praise and approve their dog's unwanted behavior, with every pet, cuddle and soothing word, I too was praising and approving Nigel's *fear* – another unwanted behavior. I should have ignored his fear from the beginning, and redirected him with some other activity. Additionally, a brisk walk to scrub off excess energy *before* a vet visit would have benefitted both of us!

TOUGH AS NAILS

Because by this time we had virtually no control over adolescent Nigel, we were not able to do some of the basic maintenance required for a dog, such as trimming his nails. He was like a greased pig – wiggly, determined, fast and strong. Frustrated, I took him to our vet's office every four weeks for nail trims and let them deal with him. But by this time, it was firmly planted in Nigel's mind that the vet was all about bad things, and he was having none of it. The flailing and screaming would begin in the parking lot and did not subside until we were back in the car and on our way home. I had no doubt that Nigel was difficult to work with for even the most seasoned vet tech, but after a particular nail trim at the vet's office that left him bleeding rather badly, I decided that I should be the one trimming his nails. Additionally, I thought that if he did not have to go there for something he hated so much, maybe he would learn to relax and not get so worked up. This began a series of plans in which I tried a variety of options to trim his nails. Yes, more plans, none of which worked. I am nothing if not tenacious and quite predictable in my approach...

"A nail trim is a highly overrated thing. I think I'll just sit out here instead."

I already knew that Nigel was terrified of the guillotine style nail clippers and I didn't blame him. I was uncomfortable using them too, so I was going to take a kinder, gentler approach – I would *file* his nails instead. I thought this idea was pure genius and I could not figure out why everyone had not gotten on to it. I purchased a large quantity of emery boards, actually clearing the rack at the pharmacy. Considering that I knew this plan was a sure winner, I would need a large supply of emery boards for the future so why not buy quantity? I tried using the roughest side of the emery board on Nigel's nails to no avail – his tough terrier nails were no match for a human's nail file! No big deal. I was sure there was something else I could use, and on the bright side, I was now stocked up on emery boards for life.

Thinking that I needed something a little more heavy duty, I purchased a wood file at the hardware store. I found out soon enough that the large file was unwieldy and difficult to control with one hand, while I held my flailing greased pig with the other. Thinking that this was a two-person job, I pulled Mike into the fray and gave him the job of holding Nigel while I tried to file, but still it was no good. I returned one last time to the guillotine style nail clipper but even with two of us, we were no match for Nigel. It seemed that we were in each other's way more than being helpful to one another. The tension caused by Nigel's flailing would begin to build and rise like clouds preceding a summer storm, resulting in us blaming each other for the process not working. I spoke with my vet about this and not surprisingly, he didn't try to talk me into bringing Nigel back to his office for nail trims. Apparently the $7 charge was not sufficient combat pay for any of his techs. Instead he suggested that I give him something to calm down before a nail trim. I left the vet's office with Acepromazine in hand, confident that I had overcome the nail trim problem once and for all. As usual, I was wrong.

I gave Nigel the sedative and waited the recommended time for the drug to take effect, and for the magic to begin. I picked up my glassy eyed, limp little dog and prepared for this to go down in nail trim history as the fastest, easiest ever. But, upon seeing the nail clipper in my hand, my drugged dog was suddenly very sober and ready to do battle, only under the influence of Acepromazine, he had lost some of his inhibitions. He was worse than ever! How could a small dog be so strong? He was more determined *not* to have a nail trim than we were to do one. Game. Set. Match. The little red dog was victorious once again. With untouched nails, he stumbled back to his bed and slept off the effects of the drug for the rest of the afternoon.

Next, I turned to my Internet Norwich Terrier discussion group. The group consists of people from around the world who are pet enthusiasts, breeders, and those who just want to learn about the breed. Someone mentioned trying a rotary grinding tool, such as a Dremel Cordless Rotary Tool. I immediately bought one and began the introductions between Nigel and the tool. Nigel was never the type of dog who was startled by unusual sounds, and thankfully he did not fear the rotary tool. He even seemed to tolerate it a little better than the guillotine-style nail clipper. But still we did not have enough control over him to complete the nail trim and effectively grind his nails to an acceptable length. I was sure that a combination of Acepromazine and the rotary tool was the answer and again, I was wrong.

What I didn't know about dogs could fill volumes (or at least this book). Overall the problem was not just Nigel. The problem was us. We had not been showing him any kind of leadership and in neglecting to do so in effect, we allowed him to become our leader. As our leader or *boss*, he took great umbrage with every attempt we made at controlling him. More on this topic coming up in the next chapter.

UH OH...

Perhaps because it seemed that almost every dog we encountered was out of control or had an owner who saw nothing wrong with their dog's obnoxious behavior, when out with Nigel, Mike began to have a subtle reaction of fear whenever we saw another dog approaching. As we walked along, suddenly I would hear him utter, "Uh oh" which is never a good thing to hear when out with your dog. With such strong feelings and expressions of fear coming from one of his people, after a while when seeing another dog approaching, Nigel would turn and head in the opposite direction. With two modes of reaction – fight or flight – when encountering fear, Nigel always chose flight. Because Nigel sensed Mike's fear, and our overall weakness, he did not trust us or look to us for protection.

Nigel was not a bad dog! Sure, he was a little hard to control when he got excited, and no, he did not always take my instruction, but at home, he was a friendly, happy, independent, and confident little dog with a delightful sense of humor. He never showed separation anxiety, nor did he destroy anything, even during the teething stages. Nigel did not bark unless there was good reason to, and he was never territorial – anyone was welcome at his home. While being independent, and even pushy with us at home, Nigel was fearful of a variety of things *outside* the home. A friend of mine had observed him and described him as "a worrier." Our lack of leadership, combined with possible natural insecurities, and lack of positive socialization experiences, were the perfect storm to create an insecure dog. This made doing new things with Nigel and participating in new activities incredibly difficult. We had within two years helped create a dog who was nervous, unable to adapt to change, and…wimpy. I often found myself frustrated about my relationship with Nigel, and I wondered, "*Why can't he adapt to anything new? Why can't he just relax and have fun? Why doesn't he trust us? What's wrong with him? How can I change him?*" I loved Nigel so much and had tried to do all the right things but somehow, so many things had gone wrong. This certainly was not what I had planned. I wanted a dog that I could take places, and have fun with. It would take me years to undo the damage we had done in a very short time.

HE'S NOT FAT… HE'S *FLUFFY*?

As mentioned in the health section in Part I of this book, there came a time that it was pointed out to me that Nigel was "obese." It all started during a regular checkup when he was about two years old. When listening to Nigel's heart, the vet kept moving his stethoscope, his brow furrowed as he concentrated. Becoming a little worried I asked, "Is everything okay?" He said, "I think I'm picking up the sound of a murmur. Just a sec." My mind searched for everything I knew about "heart murmurs" and I came up with little. He said, "I can't say for sure that it's a murmur but the sound of the flow isn't exactly normal. I think he should see a cardiologist." Concerned, I asked, "Is this serious? Is he okay?" He told me not to panic and said that a cardiologist would be the best source of testing to find out exactly what was going on with Nigel's heart. He made an appointment for him with a well-respected cardiologist at Michigan State School of Veterinary Medicine. When I returned home, I called Nigel's breeder immediately. She too was very concerned and said that she would meet us there for the appointment.

A few days later we met at MSU in Lansing, MI. The cardiologist did a number of tests, including an EKG, and some others I cannot recall all these years later. I certainly do remember the outcome of the day though. We were called into an examination room and the cardiologist entered. I am told that he is brilliant and additionally, a really a nice guy, but his serious and somewhat gruff manner was a little intimidating, especially to a novice pet owner.

Without saying a word he put up two X-rays – one of a small dog and one of a large dog. He turned to us and said, "Okay, we're going to look at a couple of X-rays here." As he pointed to the large dog's X-ray he said, "Obviously this one is not your dog. Do you see this thin shadowing over his frame?" In unison we replied, "Yes." He continued with his line of questioning, "Now, let's look at *your* dog's X-ray. Do you see this *thick* shadow over *his* little frame? See how much thicker it is than the other dog's? Do you know what that is?" He asked, as if he expected me to have the right answer. Suddenly I felt like I was in the fifth grade again, and the teacher had me in his sights. I gulped, swallowed hard, not sure if I needed to raise my hand to answer the question or not, and bravely replied, "Um... is it... *fur*?" Uh oh. I had gotten the answer wrong! He said, "No, it's fat – your dog is obese. He doesn't have a heart murmur, but his heart has to work very hard to pump blood because it is surrounded by a thick layer of fat! You have to get some weight off of him."

My face felt hot. *"Don't cry, don't cry,"* I kept telling myself as I blinked rapidly. Then, having made his point, the portly cardiologist smiled as he reached over and gently poked Mike's somewhat ample middle, and said, "Guys like us – we can control what we put into our mouths, but *he* can't, so *you* have to control what he eats. You've got to cut back on his food intake and stop giving him too many treats, and exercise him more." He added, "On a little guy like this, three or four extra pounds is a *lot* of weight – it's the difference between normal and obese. I think after you get four pounds off of him, we're going to hear a heart that sounds much more normal." The tension I felt lifted. The doctor had clearly made his point and then it was time for a little levity. He cared about Nigel's health and he knew we did too.

Nigel – both fat and fluffy. And of course begging for a treat.

Looking back on this experience and seeing the epidemic of obese dogs in the U.S., I cannot imagine how many times the cardiologist has had this conversation with pet owners over the years. He showed us a chart that illustrated how a dog is supposed to look. While standing over your dog, and looking down at him – you should see a waist. As you lightly run your hands down the length of his body, you should be able to feel his ribs without applying too much pressure. No waist and no ribs? Your dog is probably overweight.

I knew that Nigel weighed 18 pounds. Okay, 18 and *a half* pounds, but he was big for a Norwich Terrier! But *obese*? I walked him every day. I didn't think we were giving him *that* many treats, and I was certain I was feeding him the appropriate amount of food. Later, our breeder would tell me, "As soon as I saw Nigel I was pretty sure what the problem was."

Why was it that others could look at him and see what *we* didn't? As was my practice in those days, I cried all the way home, telling Nigel over and over how sorry I was and that I would make it right. The next day our regular vet called and said he had read the report and was glad that it wasn't a murmur. I said, "I'm certainly not blaming you or anything like that but, I'm curious – why didn't you ever say anything to me about Nigel's weight?" He said, "It's hard to point out things like that because people take it very personally, and we find that people get mad at *us* and go elsewhere rather than do something about it." I said, "Well, now I *am* kind of mad! I depend on your counsel and you withheld it because you *thought* I'd be mad? I can take the truth but what I can't take is thinking that you don't have my dog's best interest at heart." In the end, we both agreed that education and honesty were the best policy.

I went to the pet supply store and immediately bought a bag of "lite" food. Surely such a high profile company knew a thing or two about what was good for my dog. I began feeding Nigel his new diet food and committed to exercising him even more each day. The problem with his new food was that it seemed to leave him with little energy for more exercise, and his coat was dry and lifeless. He acted as if he was starving all the time. Surely there was a better alternative than this but what was it?

Over the next several months I continued to monitor Nigel's food intake and weight, and exercised him more, and I got his weight down to 14 pounds. Being larger than the breed standard calls for, at 12 pounds Nigel would have looked anorexic. At 14 pounds, he looked perfect. He had a waist and his ribs were easily felt even through his thick coat. We were thrilled. But still, I did not like the condition he was in. My interest in the subject of food and nutrition would continue.

~ Teachable Moment ~
My fluffy reality check.

The huge gap in the reality of how we saw Nigel and the way he truly was, has always baffled me. Why couldn't *we* see that Nigel was fat? Why was I unable to see his oh-so-wide back? Is love truly blind? Ever since the blinders were unceremoniously ripped from my eyes that day, I have been able to view my dog(s) realistically, which has been beneficial to them and to me. It is a state of reality that I highly recommend to all dog lovers for the well being of your dog.

I have also thought about why veterinarians are so hesitant to speak to owners about their dog's weight. I certainly understand that some people are not going to take it well, but if properly presented, I can't imagine someone getting hysterical and stomping out of the office. Veterinarians do not hesitate to speak up about eye problems, arthritis, or cancer. Why is that? I think it is because obesity is something that is preventable a majority of the time, and deep down, pet owners know they are responsible for it. But still I think vets are obligated to educate the owner for the pet's sake, and pet owners are obligated to hear the truth and do what is right for their pet. I want to be told the truth and I tell any new vet that. It is a great way to start a relationship based on honesty, reality, and with both parties agreeing to have the best interest of the dog at heart.

A NORWICH TALE

Common Scents – September 1999

To smell you is to love you.

I love to observe dogs. I especially love to observe them doing whatever strikes them when they aren't aware that anyone is watching them.

Recently, 1-1/2 year old Nigel was with me upstairs in the bedroom as I was getting ready for the day. Nigel was alternating between dozing and watching me go through my routine. At one point I noticed that he had gotten up and gone into our closet. I quietly left my spot at the vanity so I could observe him. There he was walking along the bottom row of my clothing, nose up, sniffing my clothes, his nubby tail wagging all the while. With each garment he sniffed it was as if he was happily greeting *me*. It was such a sweet picture of discovery but also a reminder of the power of his terrier nose. If an article of our clothing is left on the floor, Nigel will choose to sleep on it rather than any of his beds. I guess that's just another way of feeling close to the ones you love. ^..^

A NORWICH TALE

A Boy Named Justin – May 2000

Nigel shows neighborly love.

Many Norwich Terriers love children and Nigel is no exception. Daily walks through our friendly neighborhood have enabled him to meet most of the neighbors, especially kids. In Michigan everyone takes full advantage of good weather, playing outside as much as possible. There is one little boy named Justin, who Nigel seems particularly drawn to. The first time we met Justin, he was in his front yard with his mom. As we walked by, he asked if he could pet Nigel, and so we struck up a conversation with him and his mother. Justin was a sweet boy and as he gently petted Nigel he told us that his dog had recently died and that he really missed her. The look on his mother's face told us that he was taking it very hard. She said, "He just loves dogs and wants another one more than anything."

The next afternoon, my doorbell rang and there was Justin standing on my porch. I opened the door and he said, "Hi. Can Nigel come out and play?" Since his mother did not know he was coming to my house, I told him to have her call me and if she said yes, then it would be fine with me – he could come over and play with Nigel. He stood on the front porch and petted Nigel and seemed to be content to at least be near a dog for a few minutes and then he was off. A few days later, out for our usual walk, we happened upon Justin near his house riding his bike. He saw Nigel and yelled, "It's NIGELLLL!" As he awkwardly got off the bike, it was then that I noticed his left arm. It was not fully functional, and it looked a little smaller and thinner than the right one. All Nigel knew was that this was a gentle little boy who liked him and he warmly greeted his new friend, giving "air kisses."

On our daily walk a few days later, we saw Justin with several other boys on their bikes and Justin proudly pointed out, "That's my friend Nigel" as the boys got off their bikes to say hello. But Nigel only had eyes for Justin. He gave Justin his undivided attention and air kisses first, while Justin reveled in the fact that he was "Nigel's friend" all the while saying, "Yes, Nigel loves me. Nigel is my friend." After thoroughly accepting Justin's affections, only then did Nigel turn his attention to the other boys, giving air kisses – his entire body wagging all the while.

We continued to see Justin on a regular basis in the neighborhood and he even dropped by from time to time. Later that year he got a dog of his own, which he proudly brought over to meet us, but he always stopped to pet Nigel whenever he saw us out with him. Nigel continued to favor Justin over any of the other kids in the neighborhood until Justin and his family moved a few years later. I have always wondered what it was that made Justin so special to Nigel. Was it that he sensed a boy who was hurting from a loss? Was there something else that set this gentle boy apart in Nigel's keen, sensitive mind? Was it something deeper than that? This is a mystery to which only Nigel holds the answer. And he's not telling. ^..^

Chapter 7
Wonderful, Whimsical, Delightful Divot

THIS IS THE BEST TOY EVER!

It seems somewhat common that most dogs at some point will choose their "favorite" person. I have always been one to touch and pet my dogs a lot, and that was just not something that

Nigel wanted or needed. Nigel was never a dog who enjoyed laying on someone's lap, and Mike was content to allow him to lay next to him, not needing to pet him, and perhaps that was part of the reason that Nigel gravitated to him. I began to think about a dog that was more inclined to cuddle – maybe a dog that was not *so* independent.

We had stayed in contact with Nigel's breeders through phone calls and e-mail updates, visits, and sending them plenty of photos of Nigel's first three years with us. We began discussing the possibility of adding another Norwich to our family, though we were still unsure about it due to Nigel's lack of interest in, and sometimes uneasiness around other dogs. In early spring of 2001, I went to meet an eleven-month old male Norwich. The plan was that he might be good show potential but it was not meant to be. He was very cute and a very typical adolescent dog. He may have fit in beautifully in any other home but not in a home with a dog like Nigel. I wasn't sure how he would take to this energetic, confident youngster.

I told the breeder that based on Nigel's personality, this did not seem like a good fit. I felt bad. All Norwich Terriers are lovable, but he was just not a good fit energy-wise for our home. She assured me that if it did not seem right, then saying no was absolutely the right thing to do – not only for us, but for both dogs. She was confident that the right dog was out there for us.

Conversations continued about another dog, and several weeks later she mentioned a three-year old female she had decided place. Her name was Divot. I immediately recognized that unusual name – we had previously met Divot at the Detroit Kennel Club Dog Show! We both remembered her as a very sweet little black and tan Norwich girl with an adorable, friendly, but laid back personality. Yes, we would like to meet Divot again! This time we took Nigel with us. We felt that he should, and would let us know if this was a good match.

We arrived with Nigel and spent some time catching up and then it was time to meet Divot. As she came toward me, I saw the most beautiful face I had ever seen. Divot was very petite compared to Nigel. She had small, lovely, expressive deep brown eyes. She was curious, gentle, friendly, confident, and affectionate. Divot's reaction to Nigel was one of curiosity, and she gently sniffed him in all the right places. Her approach to him was calm and polite, not forceful or obnoxious. Because of her calm and gentle approach, Nigel was interested in her too, giving her a thorough sniffing. He showed no fear of Divot – she was the most well-mannered dog he had ever met! We observed the two together for a while and we all decided it was a good match. I picked her up and held her and she gently licked my cheek. We decided to bring Divot home with us that day.

Divot (L) and Nigel (R) shortly after we arrived home.
Over the years they would spend many hours sunning themselves together on these steps and in the foyer.

The ride home was not as ideal as the meeting. Poor Divot got very car sick and vomited in her crate several times. By the time we got her home she was a mess. Once home, we let the new friends wander around in the backyard for a while so that Divot could get comfortable with her new yard, and learn where to relieve herself. Divot showed no fear of being with strangers in new surroundings; she was just curious, and our wooded yard offered a tantalizing array of smells for a terrier! After a thorough exploration of her new yard, I gave her a much-needed bath and then we decided to take the new pack mates out for a walk together. Divot heeled beautifully on leash and was a joy to walk. This would be the first of many walks Nigel and Divot would take together. Later in life, when one was ill or was unable to participate, the other often refused to walk.

After our first walk together as a family, we came home, looking forward to getting to know Divot better and enjoying our first evening together. Nigel immediately jumped up on an ottoman and began to bark at her. Divot responded by ignoring him. In fact, she turned her back to him and sat down. He barked louder, looking down at her from his perch. She continued to ignore him. He jumped down from the ottoman and went into a play bow, still barking at her. Still ignoring him, she repositioned herself so that again, her back was to him. We had no idea what had gotten into Nigel. Our quiet, non-chaotic home was suddenly filled with Nigel's ear splitting barks! We were also not used to Nigel *wanting* to play with another dog. He had never sought the attention of another dog, but he desperately wanted Divot's attention! Nigel's pleas for attention went unacknowledged until sometime the following day. By then Divot's position over Nigel was in place. Now, he could be acknowledged and the fun could begin.

SCHOOL IS IN SESSION

Observing Nigel and Divot together was an amazing educational opportunity for me. Though much smaller, Divot outranked Nigel, but it was by subtle means. If Nigel was sleeping in a particular spot and she wanted it, all that was necessary was to give him "the look" and he gave up the spot immediately. Their communication seemed subtle but it was *very* clear between the two of them – they understood each other perfectly! When heading out the door, Divot always went out first. If it appeared that Nigel might consider exiting first, she gently bumped him out of the way and out the door she went. He never seemed to be offended, he just accepted it as the way things were. While Divot quickly took the dominant role over Nigel, she was very submissive to us.

Nigel had been given hundreds of toys but when we brought Divot home, he rarely played with them again. We had given him the best gift ever – Divot. At the time, I had no idea what kind of impact Divot would have on Nigel and how having her as a companion would radically improve his quality of life. I also had no idea what kind of impact Divot would have on us.

~ Teachable Moment ~
Finding the right companion for your companion.

If you already have a dog and are considering introducing another dog into your home, it is a good idea to make an honest assessment of your dog first. Consider age, temperament, level of socialization, and health. While many people believe that bringing home a puppy will put some "zip" back into their aging dog, it does not always work. I am not saying that it *will* not work, but sometimes a puppy is an annoyance to an elderly dog especially if he is ill. Know your dog's tolerances and do what is best for *him*. If your dog is a good candidate for a companion, if possible take him with you to meet a potential new dog, so he can help you make the decision. Working with an experienced breeder will go a long way in making the right decision about the right dog and this will make for a smoother transition for everyone.

Divot spots a squirrel and patiently waits for it to come closer. Nigel stands cautiously behind her.

PERFECTLY NORWICHY DIVOT

Something that fascinated me about Divot immediately, was that she possessed some very typical Norwich traits that Nigel did not. The normal Norwich Terrier bark sounds like a raspy *"Ack ack ack!"* It is a very unusual bark, which for some reason seems to perfectly fit the compact, sassy little Norwich Terrier. When Divot was trying to make me understand the urgency of something, she made a noise that can only be described as sounding like squirrel chatter, which I think is quite ironic for a terrier, but I am told that other Norwich do this too. When she was trying to get Nigel to do something, Divot would look at him and make an *"Urr urrr..."* sound. Not a growl and certainly not ferocious to me, but Nigel certainly snapped to attention. When Divot wanted something from me and was getting excited and even a little impatient, she made a different noise – one that almost sounded like she was saying *"Abba, abba, abba!"* This unusual sound was often punctuated by popping up and down for added emphasis. Popping could be done when she was either standing or sitting. Either way it was incredibly charming and hard not to give in to her demands.

Besides Divot's unique and expansive sound repertoire, when at play with Nigel she had adorable maneuvers. A quick pop and spin move always seemed to help her stay one step ahead of Nigel when they were chasing and wrestling. Once they trusted each other fully, they played endlessly, chasing each other through the house like little slot cars on an unseen track, or standing on their hind legs grappling like tiny bear cubs. Divot, while being much smaller than Nigel never backed down, and Nigel never used his much larger size to overpower her. Nigel and Divot ate side by side every day and never squabbled over food. They had an amazing bond, and a very high level of trust.

Nigel had found the best toy in the world in Divot, but she still enjoyed playing with squeaky toys, and she would bounce around the room, shaking her toy until it was "dead." Once a toy no longer squeaked, Divot saw no point in it and the toy was forgotten. One day I was observing her as she rooted through the toy basket and I realized that she had a preference when it came to her toy selection. She, a black & tan Norwich, always chose the black & tan toys and preferred them to all others. I have always been told that dogs have very limited ability to discern colors but it never failed that she chose the black and tan toys first.

Divot was the most well socialized dog I had ever met. Being around other dogs her entire life, she knew how to handle herself. She was 10-1/2 pounds of sheer confidence and terrier attitude. When meeting other dogs, whether a large or small dog, Divot handled herself with confidence and stood her ground if they were being pushy and impolite. Without a sound she signaled, *"Back off!"* Even the largest of dogs did indeed back off and respect her.

Beyond the infamous butterfly kill of his youth, Nigel seemed to posses absolutely no hunting instincts, but Divot's hunting instincts were finely tuned. When the patio door opened, she silently flew out the door, heading for the rock retaining wall around the corner of the house that also served as housing for a large population of chipmunks. Once there she remained silent, tilting her head back and forth, listening for activity within the rocks, waiting for a chipmunk to make the wrong move. Divot could also dig like nobody's business. She was strong and fast. If she thought there was subterranean vermin to be had, she was more than willing to dig for it. This was one side of Divot – brave, tenacious, tough, "verminator." The other side was an affectionate, submissive, trusting, and lovable lap dog. Divot loved to be snuggled and close to someone at all times. She was perfectly Norwichy!

Divot silently and patiently waits for a chipmunk to make a wrong move!

Nigel and Divot were the same age (she was just four months younger) yet she seemed so much more mature. The different ways in which both dogs were raised probably holds the key. Nigel was overindulged and raised by two people who were full of love but knew very little about how to raise and live with a dog. Divot on the other hand, had been raised by an experienced terrier person, who knew how to live with a pack of dogs. They could not have been more opposite in size, personality, or temperament, but they were a perfect match.

In keeping with our contract with her breeder, within a few weeks of bringing Divot home, I scheduled an appointment to have her spayed. When she came home, it was apparent that she was in a great deal of pain. We let her rest quietly in her crate and we were quite surprised to find that Nigel had appointed himself as her guardian. He lay in front of her crate, sniffing and keeping watch over her for the rest of the day. This was a side of Nigel we had not seen before and it was truly moving to see him this way. He finally had a special friend and pack mate. When bedtime came, I slept on the floor next to Divot's crate so I could listen for any signs of distress. She slept soundly through the night and by the next day she was improving, but still needed help getting around. For the next 10 nights I slept next to her crate and this seemed to be the catalyst for her choice – I was her special person. Divot became my constant companion following me everywhere, always heeling on my left side as if an invisible leash connected us. After she had completely healed from her surgery, Divot was able to sleep on our bed with us. She slept next to my side that night and every night for the rest of her life.

I WANT TO BE DIVOT

Our house happened to be the house where our large group of friends gathered so Nigel and Divot always had plenty of visitors and interaction with people. Every person who came to our home gave both dogs plenty of love and attention. Outgoing Nigel insisted upon attention, but Divot charmed everyone and drew them to her with her easy going personality and affectionate ways. Sitting at our kitchen table one day sipping coffee, a friend of Mike's looked contemplatively at sleeping Divot and said, "You know, if I ever get to come back in another life, I want to be Divot." Another friend, whose kids desperately wanted a dog, had been doing research on a variety of breeds. Frustrated because the family could not agree on which breed was the right one, he stopped by one day and as we discussed his dilemma, he took out his wallet, threw it on the table and said, "Take everything I've got in there. I want Divot." That's the kind of effect Divot had on people. She could bring out feelings in people who really did not even consider themselves to be "dog people."

A NORWICH TALE

The Canary in the Cul-de-sac – April 2002

Let's wait and see if anything happens to him...

Divot is ever confident when meeting other dogs, but she can sometimes hold back a little with new people, especially people who greet her by reaching down to pet her on the head, as most people do. She will always duck out of the way and want to sniff them first, which in the dog world is a proper greeting. One day while out on a walk, Mike noticed that Divot would approach new people only *after* Nigel had done so. As we walked on, he said, "It's like she uses him to test people first – you know, to see if they're safe." He laughed as he thought more about her technique and said, "Divot uses Nigel as her canary. He's the canary in the cul-de-sac!" This began a long running private joke whenever we were out with Nigel and Divot. ^..^

A NORWICH TALE

Let Me See! – May 2002

Watching your dog watch other things is better than watching anything else!

Divot is my TV, computer, and aquarium watcher. Perhaps her high level of interest in movement stems from her high prey drive. She loves to watch TV, especially if the program is about animals or is an animated program. She doesn't bark at the TV, she just watches in rapt fascination. When I am working at my desk, Divot is usually sitting on, or sprawled across my lap. If fascinated by something on my computer, she will attempt to climb onto the desk to get a closer look. But often she is relaxed into the crook of my arm watching me work, keeping an eye on the movements on the computer screen, until she becomes too tired and falls asleep. Though this does not make for the most comfortable working conditions for me, I wouldn't trade our arrangement for anything.

I bought an aquarium earlier this year and to say the least, Divot was thrilled with it. She stands on the chair closest to it watching intently for long periods of time, or she takes a position on the floor beneath the aquarium, one paw raised, watching the fish in total fascination. Watching Divot watch the things that fascinate her is better than watching anything else! ^..^

Watching Divot watching the fish.

Chapter 8
Follow The Leader

LOVE MAY NOT ALWAYS BE ENOUGH

While the addition of Divot to our lives brought more fun, having two dogs did add a little more chaos at times. Divot was relaxed and submissive to people, and seemed so well balanced, but with Nigel's lack of social skills and his fears, it could at times be a little trying. The difference in the two dogs made me think a lot about how they each turned out the way they did. I knew that I must be missing *something.* While I loved both Nigel and Divot very much, I lacked the ability to bring my world and Nigel's world together. I had been unable to communicate with Nigel on *his* terms. Love as it turns out was just not enough.

Being able to observe Nigel and Divot together opened up a new world for me. I was fascinated by their communication and the way they lived with one another. I was determined to learn their ways and to understand how I might incorporate some of their ways of being with each other, into *my* way of being with them. As much as I could, I began to consider everyday life from *their* perspective. I am sure that they could sense that they were very loved, but they lived in a human world with overt communication and sometimes mixed messages. Many words and gestures are used by humans to express a singular thought, whereas in a dog's world, a look or a subtle body movement makes their point perfectly clear. Not being able to previously observe Nigel communicating with other dogs (in a non-chaotic sense that is), seeing the interaction between him and Divot was an extraordinary learning experience and Divot was an experienced, and extraordinary teacher!

I began to study a variety of training methods, all claiming to be the correct one. It has been my experience that there is no such thing as a "one size fits all" approach when it comes to dogs. Each dog has a different temperament and different abilities. Add a variety of human personalities and abilities, and it gets even less predictable. Training Nigel with treats, as many methods encourage, often created chaos, as he was a little *too* food driven and his excitement about the food clouded everything else. His heightened excitement could create excitement in the usually calm Divot, and this made communicating with either dog difficult.

Considering all of this, as well as Nigel's intelligence and strong personality, I decided that the approach that made the most sense in changing and enhancing our relationship, was to create a hierarchy by showing him consistent leadership, rather than me becoming just a dispenser of treats. I was intrigued by Divot's subtle actions and her obvious ability to handle Nigel. She was never forceful, but he submitted to her lead. I decided that we needed the help of a professional. I found someone who did one-on-one in home training. With her help, I learned simple techniques to reinforce my role as leader.

The first thing we addressed was the walk. Divot, having been shown in conformation, and having lived with an experienced dog person, had beautiful leash manners, but that meant little when Nigel didn't, and I was trying to walk them together. Pulling a dog only creates a dog that pulls even harder. A properly placed collar, meaningful correction, and keeping Nigel focused on me, was our key to success. I put away the 16-foot retractable leash I had previously used, and got a six-foot leash, and I taught Nigel to walk politely at my side. A walk was begun only when he was calm. I learned how to get his attention and keep it, and to think of the leash as an extension of me, and a direct line of communication with him. Having Nigel walk *with* me and Divot, (not pulling us), made walking a much more pleasurable experience. Having your dog next to you is much safer than letting him walk ahead of you, as discarded gum, candy, or other carelessly tossed items are easy for a dog to snatch up when he is nowhere near you.

The other thing I wanted to address was mealtimes, which could often be loud and a little chaotic, with Nigel barking demandingly for his food. Within a short time, *both* dogs were barking and demanding food. Since I was the leader, and all good things should come from my hand, they would now have to *earn* their food. Rather than allow them to jump on me, barking demandingly, I instructed them to sit quietly while I prepared their food. Any demanding behavior was met with "Ah ah ah!" If that didn't settle them down, I repeated "Ah ah ah!" and walked away, making them wait even longer. Eventually, hearing "Ah ah ah!" was enough to settle them down. They learned not to be pushy lest I walk away. Soon, I was able to prepare their meal and put their bowls down while they sat patiently. Only when I said, "Okay" could they approach their bowls and eat.

Our trainer explained that dogs can be overwhelmed by too much input. Sometimes an excited owner will inadvertently give a variety of mixed signals including a string of verbal commands and confusing body language. She suggested that we talk less, think about, and use body language to communicate with Nigel, just as Divot did. I had to admit that besides our lack of confidence in our own leadership, we often did overwhelm the already excited Nigel with a great deal of excited dialog.

Once I understood the basic philosophy and saw Nigel's positive response, my confidence grew and I began to try more things. There are a variety ways to show leadership to your dog in common, everyday occurrences around the house. Another example of an everyday situation that can easily become chaotic with an excited dog, is the act of answering the door. This is a problem for many people, and with a small dog like a Norwich Terrier, an open door is an easy escape, and when you have two small dogs, it's even more problematic. My new way of handling the door situation was to get them away from the door. But, rather than reaching for their collars and physically removing my excited little dogs from the door (remember, pulling = *more* pulling), I learned to use body blocks and hand gestures to walk them back from the door – essentially causing them to remove *themselves* from the area of the door. Once they had removed themselves, I gave the stay command. They could stand or sit, but they had to stay away from the door. This has worked well over the years both at home and in hotel rooms. Later, when we lived in Arizona, I created a new behavior, by giving Nigel and Divot a treat in the kitchen whenever the doorbell rang. Soon, the ringing doorbell sent them running to the kitchen to their special place – their rug.

I worked on the "come" command by calling Nigel and Divot to me, but calling them *only* for something great such as a treat or a walk. If I needed them to come to me for something unpleasant such as a nail trim, I never called them using that command. Outside I used a long line to help overcome distractions, and soon Nigel's reliability with the come command was excellent. Divot, having a higher prey drive, took a little more work to keep focused. Later I would add a clicker for maximum focus when off-leash hiking. Both dogs were extremely reliable and trustworthy, which for terriers in the woods, is no small feat.

Overall, my goal in all of this was to make Nigel understand that I was now his leader and he was my follower. In following me, like Divot, he had nothing to worry about! I learned a great deal from our training sessions and over the years, I used this way of thinking to create other behaviors I wanted.

Indulge me as I veer off for a moment... When discussing the leader and follower roles some people get a little squeamish about the topic and for some reason have come to believe that leadership equates to cruel domination, with no use of any positive reinforcement. That is not the way I view it or have implemented it. My view of showing leadership to a dog uses a family with children as an example. In my opinion, without clarity of roles, you create chaos and a search for leadership and security. In my mind that is how it should work with my dogs. If I am providing leadership, they do not have to take on that stressful role. By meeting all of their needs, I am showing leadership. This gives them security. Their role is to trust and follow. If I am confident and consistent, and give meaningful direction, they *will* follow.

Though removed as "top dog," Nigel nevertheless kept his throne – his favorite window seat. He and Divot enjoyed watching over their yard from this comfy perch for many years.

If you are uncomfortable with words like "leader" or "follower" or "submission" or "dominance," then it just might be that you are uncomfortable with the true nature of dogs. All dogs show submission or dominance – both wild canids as well as our domestic companions. This is made clearer when you have two dogs in your household. Add a third dog it usually becomes even more apparent. Our adorable, lovable little bed buddies are *animals* and their ways are not our ways. We are all the wiser when we remember that and live with them in ways they can understand. That said, when you accept the fact that your dog is indeed an animal, and you consider the deep bond that can be created between human and dog, it makes the relationship even more amazing and special!

As I began to change my way of relating to Nigel and reshaped him into a follower, his trust in me grew, and he seemed more relaxed. It was as if I had lifted a burden from him. But as it always happens, there is more to the story, and always more things we can learn about our dogs and ourselves.

NAIL TRIMS PART II

Nail trim morning was upon us. With my new role of leader in place, we set out for a long walk because a tired dog is a good dog, especially in a stressful situation. When we returned home, I got out the Dremel tool and Mike and I prepared to do Nigel's nails. Nigel did not fight as hard as he had in the past but he still fought, making it difficult to get his nails to an acceptable length. As usual, the clouds of tension between Mike and I began to build. Finally I said, "Let me try this by myself." This was a suggestion Mike did not argue with. I took Nigel back out for a short walk alone, to "restart" the process and when we came back, I confidently placed him on the grooming table without a word, and started working on his nails. Did he struggle? Yes, a little, but when he protested I shushed him and calmly continued, ignoring his dramatic show. I did not stop! I knew he was not in pain. This was purely an emotional outburst that he had learned was an effective way to get us to stop. Within a few minutes he realized that his tactics no longer worked and he gave up and submitted to the process. About 15 minutes later we were finished. He had short nails, with no bleeding, and I was thrilled that I had successfully done what I thought was impossible! I celebrated with Nigel, praising him for what *really* was good behavior!

As I shared my victory with Mike I asked him what his thoughts were on why it turned out that ultimately it was easier for me to do the nail trim without him. I asked him how *he* felt about helping with the nail trims. He replied, "I hate it. I dread it. I know it has to be done but I feel sorry for him. I don't like seeing him be that scared." And the light bulb burned a little brighter! Nigel's overreaction to nail trims may have been based on his own fear, and in the beginning his lack of trust in us, but an important component that had been overlooked was Mike's feelings about the situation, something Nigel easily sensed. If the human was upset about the situation, maybe he should be too.

This was my introduction to how our strong emotions affect how our dogs respond to us. Even though I had usurped his role as leader, Nigel was *still* reacting to Mike's nervousness. When the negative stimulus (Mike) was removed, Nigel had less to react to. You have probably heard it said that dogs "smell fear." Fear per se, doesn't actually have an odor, but perspiration does, and so does adrenaline as it is suddenly injected into our bloodstream when we are frightened. When a human feels nervous, fearful, or another highly charged emotion, and the body reacts, a dog can sense that change. Going back a little further, when we were out walking with Nigel, and Mike saw an unruly dog coming toward us, his fear of what *might* happen (nothing ever did), caused Nigel to react – he would stop and go the other way. The communication Nigel was getting from Mike told him that there was something to fear, and he reacted to it accordingly. Once fears were acknowledged and dealt with, we started down a long road of reprogramming ourselves, and then our dog. With knowledge and the acquisition of new skills, we were headed toward a better and more successful life with both Nigel and Divot!

~Teachable Moment ~
Let's play "Follow the Leader"!

I had read books on training – some basics of how to get your dog to sit, stay, or come, (in the early days of training, Nigel often took many of my training commands as mere *suggestions*), but I had never read anything on how dogs are wired – how *they* might see and react to the world around them. All dog lovers are cognizant of the fact that their dogs are not children in furry suits, but on a subconscious level, that is sometimes how people approach their relationship with their dog. They try to relate to him as they would a human child. I believe this is simply out of ignorance or inexperience as was the case with us. While these are good intentions and based on love, this approach does not fulfill the dog's needs, and can create behavior problems due to lack of effective communication.

If your dog feels secure with you and with his place in the world, there is no reason he should not be a happy and well-adjusted member of your family. This is something I learned unfortunately *after* Nigel was firmly ensconced in his leadership role. In our domestic situation, a puppy's mother provides the initial leadership role for her puppies. When a puppy comes to us, we should fill that role and continue the teachings that his mother started, so that our pup can mature with a sense of security, and a clear understanding of what is acceptable and what is not. A mother feeds and grooms her pups, and she plays with them too, but when they get out of line, she clearly and firmly puts them back in line. Sometimes it is with a push, a growl, or even a snap! She doesn't attack them, she is simply using the tools she has. The puppy's mother teaches her pups everything they need to know without using a single word or command. There are no treats in *her* training class! She instructs by using her whole being – her instinctual brain and her body. When a frightened pup comes running back to his mother his fear is not rewarded – his mother's confidence and attitude to the stimulus become his confidence and attitude. Breeding an insecure female means her pups will learn her insecure ways of coping with stress. This is why breeding only well balanced dogs is so important! Remembering this lesson from nature and keeping our emotions in check will help in raising a secure, confident puppy!

~Teachable Moment ~
Heeling Words

In my opinion, when it comes to walking dogs, there are no hard and fast rules about which side your dog should walk on. I am an American, and for some reason, though we drive and walk on the right side, we've adopted a left side heel for our dogs. This is all fine and well for every day outings in the neighborhood, but what about a day out in a high foot traffic area? When you are on the right side of the sidewalk with your dog heeling on your left, this puts him directly in the path of everyone you pass by. While perhaps not problematic for a large dog, a small dog such as a Norwich, can easily be accidently kicked or stepped on. He would be safer and probably more comfortable on your right, so why not train him that it is okay to heel on either side of you? (I know you traditionalists are cringing right now.) Try applying the same flexibility when walking two dogs. If having them both heel on the same side of you creates a competition of one dog trying to get out in front of the other, simply put one dog on *each* side of you to avoid tension. Make choices that actually work for you and your dogs!

~Teachable Moment ~
Loving hugs or dominant displays?

Being able to observe Nigel and Divot together was an amazing learning experience, and over the years, I would continue my studies and observances, always seeking to better understand my dogs, and equally as important, to be better understood by them. After Divot had joined our family, I read an amazing book that really opened my eyes to understanding the differences between us and our dogs. This new understanding changed even more, my way of being with my dogs, especially Nigel.

The book was The Other End Of The Leash by Patricia McConnell, Ph.D. Among the myriad of ways humans and dogs differ, in the book Dr. McConnell points out the difference between human greetings and canine greetings as one example. We humans greet one another straight on, with good eye contact, sometimes including a handshake or a hug. In the dog world however, most of the aforementioned could be taken as a show of dominance, aggression, or at least, rude behavior! As someone who comes from a long line of huggers, I found the section on hugging to be very eye opening. Dr. McConnell writes, "Except for humans, chimpanzees and bonobos are the huggers of the animal kingdom, hugging one another when they are excited, happy, anxious, or downright terrified." Regarding humans hugging dogs she writes, "... while they were thinking warm, loving thoughts, their dog interpreted their hug as a rude, domineering threat display."[1] To emphasize her point, Dr. McConnell includes photos of blissfully happy people hugging dogs that look unhappy, tense, or annoyed. These two examples from Dr. McConnell's book highlight just the tip of the iceberg of how different we two species really are!

Just as I did when puppy proofing my house – getting down on a puppy's level to look at the world from his perspective – I began to dog proof my relationship with my dogs by trying to look at our relationship from *their* perspective. Training a dog to follow some basic commands was one thing but knowing how to relate to them in terms that were natural and non-offensive to them was quite another!

Though I was not feeling well, it is Nigel and Divot who look most comfortable and the ones getting rest! Note that Divot is very much at ease being on her back and close to me, while Nigel chooses to be next to me, facing away. Each has a very different comfort zone!

While submissive Divot never minded being close or even being gently hugged, after reading Dr. McConnell's book, as difficult as it was, I stopped trying to hug Nigel because clearly it made him uncomfortable. By hugging Nigel, I was meeting my human need to express my love for him, but by doing so in my human way, I was not meeting *his* needs. My dogs have always had excellent eye contact with me, which is a sign of their confidence. Getting too close to Nigel's face however, and that kind of intense, close contact made him terribly uncomfortable and he always moved away. For dogs, there is good eye contact and there is "in your face" eye contact, the latter, again possibly interpreted as a display of dominance, aggression, or at least rudeness. Nigel, not being the most submissive of dogs, and certainly not a dog who wanted face to face closeness, never gave "kisses," the way Divot did, and I had to accept that. Wanting to do what was best for Nigel, I found other ways to express my love for him by doing things he truly did enjoy such as rubbing his chin, his ears, and his rump. Since gentle hugs and close facial contact did not seem to make Divot uncomfortable, my way of being with her was much different.

I would urge everyone to please consider Dr. McConnell's observations, not just to create a better relationship with your dog, but consider it for your own safety. I cringe when I see a parent let their child to run up to a dog and hug it, especially when it is a dog they do not know. Never get face to face with a dog, especially a dog you do not know really well. Remember, the affection you mean to show, and the meaning the dog interprets can be very different!

By learning the *ways* of dogs, I began to enjoy a much more successful and happier coexistence with them. Having this information would serve me well as years later I operated a successful "Pet Nanny" business and dealt with a variety of breeds, and temperaments.

TAKE TWO!

Divot was an incredibly easy dog to live with and being so confident and well socialized she was a joy to take places. I enjoyed having a dog to do things with, but I was not satisfied with just taking Divot with me – I wanted Nigel to experience different things too. I was certain that his life would be so much more interesting if I could get him comfortably into more social situations. This desire to include Nigel in more aspects of my life started us on a journey that would eventually turn Nigel from a homebody into dog on the go!

I first began by taking Nigel and Divot to a beautiful trail system that we had in the area. Walking and biking were permitted on the paved pathways, and in summer, it was extra lovely with giant trees providing a canopy of dappling shade. Our first outing seemed to go well, as Nigel seemed eager to get out of the car and explore. It was a weekday morning and the trail was mostly void of people. We came across a few moms with strollers and some runners, but no one with dogs, so the outing was only positive experiences. It could not have gone any better in my mind. Filled with confidence in myself, we went back the next day. Nigel, who had the uncanny ability to always know where he was, burst into excited barking when I turned into the parking lot for the trailhead. Pleased that he was happy to be out and experiencing something new and fun, I cheerfully talked to the dogs as I got them out of the car. "You guys wanna go for a walk? Yeah – let's go for a walk!"

I did not realize that again, I was praising what was, and what would become an unwanted behavior. Was Nigel happy? I didn't know for sure. Was he nervous? I wasn't sure about that either. Was he excited? I thought so. Was he nervous *and* excited? Now, *that* was a big possibility. Was he being demanding? That too was a possibility. I did not know what any of his behavior meant, yet I was praising him for it and approving it. I made the mistake in thinking that excited barking was a good thing, perhaps indicating happiness, so I did not correct it but instead I unfortunately reinforced it. I continued to take Nigel and Divot to the walking trail, to the parks, and to the pet supply stores. Nigel's confidence seemed to grow as he got used to participating in new experiences, even meeting other dogs. But much to my embarrassment, we were the vehicle pulling into the parking lot with the obnoxious little dog barking frantically in the back seat. Once out of the car though, Nigel was quiet and well behaved.

I must confess, all these years and hundreds of outings later, the barking bursts are the one thing that I have not been able to correct. Our entry into a parking lot always reminds me of the movie Speed. The story took place on a city bus that was rigged with explosives; the explosives were set to detonate if the bus slowed to a speed under 50 m.p.h. That is a lot like traveling with Nigel. Keep a steady speed and he is fast asleep, but slow down to turn into a parking lot and Nigel detonates.

~Teachable Moment ~
Your dog makes great reading material.

As you have just read, I missed a perfect opportunity to stop what would become an ongoing problem and an unwanted behavior, when I pulled into that trailhead parking lot the second time around. Because I was not skilled at reading Nigel's body language, or understanding his vocal cues, I failed to see the reality of the situation and unfortunately reinforced a behavior I certainly did not want. Learning how to read body language takes understanding and practice. For our dogs this kind of communication comes naturally and observing them can go a long way getting educated!

Going back to our first parking lot entry, I wrote that Nigel "seemed eager to get out" and for the second outing, I thought he "seemed happy." In reality, that observation was probably incorrect. An excited dog is not necessarily a *happy* dog. For all I know, and as history would dictate, Nigel was probably nervous, excited, demanding, or a little of all three. Rather than waiting for him to calm down, I rewarded him by talking excitedly to him (approval to a dog), getting him out of the car (rewarding him) and taking him for a walk on the trail (approval and reward). By the second outing, he was out of control. Had I known better, I would have corrected the unwanted behavior by waiting for him to calm down and *then* rewarded him with a walk on the trail for being calm and quiet. Actions and ignorance have consequences!

A WEBSITE IS BORN

In late 2001 Mike came to me with an idea: a website for Nigel and Divot. By this time the Internet was a huge part of most everyone's daily life. I had no idea why Nigel and Divot needed a website, but he continued to encourage me to consider it. He reminded me about how difficult it was for us to find information on the Norwich Terrier breed when we began our research. He encouraged me to share what I had learned about the breed, including tales about life with Nigel and Divot, and of course some of our beautiful photos. Mike discussed the idea with his friend and webmaster, Donnie Fischer, and he was instantly on board and excited about the project. Norwich Tales launched in the spring of 2002 and was warmly received by those who love Norwich Terriers and those who were interested in learning more about the breed as a potential pet.

Nigel and Divot even received "fan mail" on a regular basis. The Norwich Tales website has been a fantastic experience, enabling me to meet, speak with, or enjoy e-mail dialog with people from across the country, and around the world. Isn't it just like dogs to bring people together?

A NORWICH TALE

Who Says Dogs Don't Think Logically? – April 2003

Nigel applies problem-solving principles to get what he wants.

Every morning I walk on my treadmill, which is in our basement family room. Every morning Nigel and Divot accompany me and get a "chewie" (bully stick) as part of our routine. Usually at some point during their chewing ritual, a silent signal is given and they suddenly switch chewies. Their signal is so subtle, I have never detected it but, like a well-choreographed dance, they get up at precisely the same time and make the switch. But there have been rare occasions when Divot decides not to make the exchange, and she continues to chew her stick, ignoring Nigel's intense stares. He inches closer and closer to her staring intently, hoping to initiate the exchange, sometimes with success, but sometimes to no avail. I have realized however, that while he is staring at her, he is also plotting…

One particular morning when Divot chose yet again not to participate in the usual bully stick exchange, and Nigel's prolonged staring had failed to motivate her to do so, he seemed to abandon the idea and ran upstairs. After a few moments, he barked from the top of the stairs, and Divot, being curious ran up to see what he was barking at. As she ran up the stairs, he passed her on the way down, and pounced upon her bully stick. Poor Divot was confused, still looking to find the cause of his barking up there. He continued to use this tactic for a few days but she finally caught on. After that, his barks would be acknowledged by Divot, but with her bully stick held firmly in her mouth, as she looked up at him from the bottom step. Nigel, never one to take defeat easily, was forced to come up with a new diversionary tactic.

It was a few weeks later when he unveiled the new plan. I was on the treadmill, and both dogs were enjoying their bully sticks. Nigel was prepared for the exchange but once again, Divot was not cooperating in their unspoken agreement. Nigel then trotted to the patio door and pawed at it, one of his signals to be let out. I stopped the treadmill and went to open the door for him. Divot, never missing an opportunity to catch a squirrel or chipmunk off guard, ran full speed out the open door, pushing past Nigel as she went. That was okay, he had no intention going out anyway. He ran back to the bully sticks and chose the one she had abandoned and settled in to enjoy a good, long chew. You could almost sense his delight with himself for pulling *that* off. Divot may not be the problem solver that Nigel is, but she is a smart dog and after a few days of this, she caught on to this new tactic too. Her curiosity still got the best of her, but when the door opened, her bully stick went out *with* her. Weeks went by, but tenacious Nigel was not prepared to give up yet, and his next tactic was a personal blow to me as I was used in his scheme.

Nigel possesses many of the traits of his cousin, the Norfolk Terrier. He is a brilliant problem solver, and is not the kind of dog who wants cuddling and petting all the time, usually only on *his* terms. So, the morning he unveiled his newest plan, we were well into our routine – me on the treadmill and Nigel and Divot settled in with their bully sticks. Nigel was ready to make the switch, but once again, Divot was not willing. After a few minutes of unsuccessful staring, Nigel approached the side of the treadmill with his ears down submissively, his nubby tail wagging, and with a look in his eyes that said to me, *"I really love you. Pet me please!"* Taken in by his overture of affection, I stopped the treadmill to pet and scratch him, glad for his desire for attention. Divot's jealousy over this little scene got the best of her and she dropped her bully stick and came over for some attention too. As you have probably guessed, while I was petting and speaking lovingly to both of them, Nigel slipped away and took Divot's bully stick. Such is life with a brilliant dog. ^..^

Chapter 9

The Good Life

THE LIFE AND TIMES OF NIGEL AND DIVOT

Life for Nigel and Divot was good. They had plenty of fresh air and exercise, they enjoyed fun outings, and they were loved immensely. We too were enjoying life with our fun little terriers. Having two dogs was not as difficult as we thought it would be once we had gained a better understanding of our little canine friends, and Nigel and Divot adored each other. Each day was a delight as they amused us with their antics and their quirky personalities. They brought an incredible amount of love and laughter to our home and they were at the center of our lives. The more we learned about living with dogs, life just kept getting better and better!

WHAT'S FOR DINNER?

One day I was talking to a friend and we were discussing a health issue her dog was having. She brought up a woman by the name of Marina Zacharias whom she called a "holistic practitioner." Never having heard of such a thing, I asked what a "holistic practitioner" was and what they did. Later, I did an Internet search for Marina and one of the first things I found was an article she had written, which would forever change my thinking about another topic – food. The article was called "Food For Thought" and it was followed by another called "It's In the Bag." These articles brought to light the questionable ingredients in some commercial dog foods, and called into question their healthfulness. After reading these enlightening articles, I was forced to reexamine what I was feeding Nigel and Divot.

While I had managed to get the excess weight off Nigel with a weight control dry food, it was proving difficult to keep the weight off despite increased exercise, and still, I did not like the condition of his coat. Also of concern, my sweet, snuggly Divot had a terrible odor. She often smelled like a dirty gym sock. Additionally, her coat and skin felt greasy. A Norwich Terrier should not be bathed frequently (some would say if at all) but at least for the first few days following a bath, she smelled a little fresher. The odor would always return though.

As I continued to read about diet, I learned how food affects each system of the body. Some outward signs of an unsuitable diet include among other problems, itchy skin, greasy skin and coat, accompanied by odor. By bathing Divot I could temporarily cover the problem, but that was not addressing the real problem, which was from *within*. I decided to "detox" Nigel and Divot for 30 days with a basic home made diet. I continued to feed them a homemade diet for a few months and, eventually I began feeding them a raw diet. The results were amazing! They were energetic, both had excellent weight that was easy to maintain, beautiful teeth, and beautiful coats, and Divot no longer had the odor she once had! In fact, neither dog smelled like *anything*.

I never went back to the big name brand food I had once thought was the best. I continued feeding Nigel and Divot a raw diet for many years, but later, when we traveled with them, this would present a problem. Switching from raw to kibble for travel was not difficult when they were younger – they adjusted to the change easily – but as they aged, their digestive systems were not so eager for that much change. Over the years I have fed a homemade diet, a raw diet, and kibbles made by smaller "holistic" minded manufacturers. Nigel and Divot did well on all three types of diet. When feeding kibble, I additionally offer fresh meat, vegetables, fruit, yogurt, and fish oil. I change foods, transitioning slowly, after two small bags.

~Teachable Moment~
Thoughts for food.

Looking back at the issue of Nigel's weight, the first mistake I probably made in feeding him was that I had been feeding him according to the chart on the bag of food. If you do that, it is highly likely that you will be overfeeding your dog, which is bad for your dog but good for dog food sales. My breeder had instructed me to feed an adult Norwich 1/3 cup of food, twice a day, but it seemed like such a small amount! Surely Nigel needed more food. Wrong! I learned not to be static with the amount of food Nigel and Divot would get each day. For a low activity day, less food is necessary for your dog. For a high activity day of walking several miles and lots of play, more food is necessary. If you are doing a lot of training and using treats, those too must be calculated into meal amounts. Another mistake I made was thinking that the biggest brand names mean the absolute best food. A high profile name, does not necessarily guarantee the best food for your dog. Cheap grain fragment fillers are empty calories that offer no benefits to your dog.

I am not an expert on canine nutrition, so I am not going to tell you what you should or should not feed your dog. I do encourage you to educate yourself on the production of, and the ingredients in commercial dog foods. Learn to read labels, and then make informed decisions on what is best for your dog.

~Teachable Moment~
Norwich-proofing your kitchen.

Sharing every aspect of your life with a dog is truly a rewarding experience. Sometimes however, food preparation time can become a little chaotic if you allow your dog's behavior and zeal for food to go unchecked. I am not just talking about when you are preparing *his* food, I am talking about preparing *your* food! Sometimes in Nigel's youth I found myself becoming frustrated because he was often underfoot in the kitchen. Back then, other than crating him, I did not know how to fix the problem. When we added Divot to our family, I then had two little beggars under foot. I have always set aside vegetables or other healthy tidbits for Nigel and Divot when preparing our food, and I know that it was this association and expectation that contributed to their constant presence underfoot. One day though, it was made very clear to me that stumbling over them while annoying, was not the worst thing that could happen. As I was preparing dinner, I accidentally knocked a pair of kitchen shears onto the floor. Thankfully neither dog was standing where the shears fell, but it scared me enough to do something about the problem immediately. After some thought, I came up with a solution that has served us well over the years.

I did not want to ban Nigel and Divot from the kitchen, but I wanted to make sure that they were safe while I was cooking, so I created a "safety zone" for them. I bought a medium size rug and placed it away from my food prep area, but in a place where they could still see me. That evening before I began to prepare dinner, I put Nigel and Divot on the rug and gave the "stay" command. They could sit, stand, or lie down – any posture was acceptable, as long as they stayed on the rug. The rug provided both a visual and physical boundary so to speak, which made it easier for them to understand what I was asking of them. For staying on the rug, I would occasionally walk over and give them a tidbit of something. Attempting to move off the rug was met with "Ah ah ah" and the offender was returned to the rug. Soon enough, they learned that their rug was the best place to be in the kitchen because yummy treats were given there and nowhere else. Most important to me was that they were safe.

Previously I had worked with them to remove themselves from the door when someone arrived, rather than pulling them away. This idea was similar. Rather than crating Nigel and Divot, or constantly removing them from the kitchen, this technique allowed them to remove themselves from underfoot. Staying on the rug was not only safe, but a nicely rewarded mental exercise!

A NORWICH TALE

Nigel & Divot Beat the Winter Blahs – January 2004

Building a makeshift agility course.

There is an old saying in Michigan, "If you don't like the weather, just wait five minutes – it'll change." Often that did seem to be the case, except in winter, when unfortunately it did not seem to change that much at all. West Michigan winters could be counted on to be cloudy, snowy, and cold for months on end. Still, at least once a day, I would bundle up, and take Nigel and Divot out for some kind of outing. Occasionally, though some days were just too cold for any of us to be outside (okay, for *me* to be outside), but with two young, energetic terriers, what can one do on a cold winter day?

Build a mini makeshift agility course of course! The idea came to us after seeing some great photos of Norwich doing agility. Using some boxes from a recent purchase, we created our mini course in the basement family room. One of the boxes was about 10 feet long and made a perfect tunnel. A smaller box could serve as a mini tunnel, and an excellent, non-threatening introduction to the tunnel experience. A spare dowel from a finished project, would serve as a jump. As we set up our mini agility course, Nigel and Divot were of course in the mix, so introducing them to these new additions to the family room was a piece of cake. Or in this case, a piece of chicken!

With Mike at one end of the short tunnel holding Divot, and me at the other end with the chicken, when called, she ran through with no hesitation and received her chicken and praise. Not sure about this whole thing, but after learning that there was a food-based benefit to going through the short tunnel, Nigel soon followed Divot through, and received his reward for his bravery. Once they understood that the little tunnel was a very rewarding experience, we moved on to the longer tunnel. The longer tunnel proved to be a little more of a psychological challenge for them but with their terrier instincts, and the promise of chicken, they quickly overcame any hesitations. Once the tunnels had been mastered, we moved on to the jump. At first the dowel was placed on the floor so they could step over it. Then we made it more challenging by placing a book under each end, eventually moving to such incredible heights as a small can of soup!

With Mike taking turns holding each dog, I was able to focus and allow each to "run the course" with me. Then, we switched, so I could work with the other. With his lunch hour over, Mike had to go back to work so it was up to me to continue. Getting them to follow me over the jump was easy. Without Mike to hold them at the entrance of the tunnel however, they usually ran straight to me avoiding the tunnel altogether, and jumped about, pleased with their performance, still expecting their treat. With one human and two dogs trying to do the same activity, it was utter chaos but what a fun way to spend a cold, snowy afternoon! ^..^

A NORWICH TALE

Nigel's Bathtub Tale – December 2004

He's so smart it's scary.

Several weeks ago we took a weekend trip to Florida to attend the wedding of a friend. Our friend Kathy came to stay with Nigel and Divot while we were gone. The background of this story is not very funny but it is relevant to the story of Nigel's actions, which were funny.

Several weeks before our planned trip, Kathy was bitten by a relative's dog. After fourteen stitches and heavy-duty antibiotics, it was no surprise that she wasn't feeling well. She had a terrible reaction to the antibiotics, one of the reactions being an itchy skin rash. A baking soda bath seemed a good idea to soothe her skin (she later found out it wasn't), but her bathtub was not deep enough for a therapeutic soak, so I suggested she come over and use mine. Nigel loves to lie next to the bathtub when someone is soaking – it is something he has done since he was a pup. He loves Kathy too so the day she came over for a soak, he was one happy dog.

So, that's the not-so-nice background of the story. We left for our trip early in the morning. When I spoke to Kathy a little later that day she was at our house and assured me that everything was fine. Nigel and Divot were very happy to see her, but she had a Norwich Tale of her own to tell. She explained that after a robust greeting from both dogs, Nigel ran upstairs and sat on the landing looking down at her. She called him to come down but he wouldn't come to her. She called him again but he stayed put, just staring down at her. Then he looked back toward our bedroom. Finally, not understanding why he wouldn't come to her but sure he had a concern up there, she went upstairs to see what he was trying to tell her. Pleased that she had finally come to him, he walked her right to the bathroom and sat next to the bathtub, and looked up at her. It took her a moment to realize what he was thinking. It was as if he was saying, *"Are we going to take a bath again today?"* She said, "I couldn't believe it – he's just too smart!" She told him no, that they weren't going to take a bath. Getting that clarified, he came back downstairs with her and they all enjoyed their long weekend together. ^..^

~Teachable Moment~
Avoiding a slippery slope.

One blustery winter evening as we were coming in from a potty outing, Divot slipped on the track of the patio door. The track was wet, and that, combined with her wet feet, caused her to slip as she jumped over the threshold. After drying eight little feet with a towel I always kept by the door, we headed upstairs but Divot wouldn't follow. I encouraged her to come up but still, she wouldn't come, and instead, sat at the bottom of the stairs. I went back downstairs to encourage her to come up with me, but she was unwilling to try, and instead, just looked unnerved about going near the stairs. Wanting to help her but not wanting to encourage her new fear, I decided to take her back outside and see if that might reset her brain. It didn't. Instead of coming in, she just stood pitifully at the door, imploring me to help her.

I brought her in and pondered the problem. After a few minutes, I realized that the towel was the answer! I placed the towel on the track of the patio door. I took Divot back outside and placed her front paws on the dry towel and she bounded in the door! I repeated the process a few more times until she fully regained her confidence, and then walked to the stairs and went up. Success! She bounded up the stairs with me as if nothing had ever happened! For a few more outings I placed the towel on the threshold for her, just to make sure there was no chance of her slipping, and then I stopped using it. Never again did Divot show any hesitation about coming in the door no matter the weather conditions.

Had I gone the easy route, I could have carried Divot upstairs, but there is a good possibility that she would never have been willing to climb or descend stairs again on her own. When your dog suddenly develops a new fear, do not encourage it with praise, petting, or "just do it for her." Instead, try to work through it as soon as possible to "reset" the brain and restore confidence!

GO WEST YOUNG DOGS!

Once we learned some basic dos and don'ts of taking Nigel and Divot on outings, we continued to expose them to a variety of situations, all of us becoming more comfortable and confident with the practice we were getting. At the time, I had no idea how important this practice would be.

I lure cautious Divot into Lake Michigan with a piece of baby carrot.

In the winter of 2004 the economy in Michigan was beginning to show signs of weakness. Being self-employed as an independent contractor, Mike knew he had to start looking for other business opportunities. Soon enough, a new opportunity presented itself, but it was not in Michigan, it was in Arizona.

We had visited the state years before and found the climate to be very agreeable. It was very different from the clouds and harsh winters we were used to in Michigan. After giving it much thought, and making several visits to the area, we decided to take a chance and make the move. Even with the advances we had made with Nigel, there was still one big hurdle to overcome – traveling across country with a dog who had never traveled any distance before, or spent a night in a hotel room.

In early June of 2005, we said good-bye to our families, friends and neighbors, our beautiful home, our much-loved neighborhood, and everything familiar, and we headed off with Nigel and Divot to a new life in the Southwest. Both dogs did really well on the trip. When we pulled into the parking lot of our hotel that first evening, as usual, Nigel had his outburst, but afterward, he was calm and even slept through the night. Divot of course, took it all in stride. She could sleep anywhere. This cross-country move – this uncharted territory – turned out to be the first of many trips we would take with Nigel and Divot!

Chapter 10
Midwest to Southwest

WHAT'S WITH ALL THE ROCKS?

The desert is home to many strange creatures. Having grown up watching the cartoon adventures of Wile E. Coyote and the Road Runner, it was strange to find ourselves with these creatures as our neighbors. It was not unusual to see the distinct shape of the Road Runner, well, doing just that – *running across the road!*

Sedona, Arizona is one of the most beautiful places on earth. With its unique red rock formations, it almost seems other-worldly. Some of the rock formations have taken on their own "personalities" and are aptly named such things as Coffee Pot Rock, Snoopy Rock, Bell Rock, and the awe inspiring Cathedral Rock to name a few. Sedona is truly a must-see for everyone. We had always loved the unique, red beauty of the area and we settled in a small community just outside of Sedona, with views of the famous red rocks from our back yard. Nigel and Divot adjusted amazingly well to their new home and surroundings, and made many friends in our new neighborhood. The eco friendly stone yards of the area were the complete opposite of the soft green grass and abundant trees they were used to in Michigan. Their once soft, lush green world, was replaced by a hard, brown and red world, that at times, could be unforgiving to little paws.

The activity they seemed to enjoy the most in their new environment, was hiking amongst the beautiful red rocks of Sedona. With our newfound confidence in being out and about with them, we hiked most of the trails in Sedona with Nigel and Divot at our side. At seven years of age, our hardy little dogs had no problem hiking miles of trails with us. Often people would stop us and ask about them, which enabled us to meet interesting people from all over the world, all because they were curious about our happy, hardy, friendly little terriers. Sometimes we would take along our backpacks, and picnic amongst the red rocks. Other times after hikes we would stop for a bite to eat at one of the many outdoor eateries in Sedona, with Nigel and Divot joining us, sitting under our table. Another new experience added to their list of "can do!"

PLACES TO GO PEOPLE TO SEE...

With a variable topography ranging from 8,000 foot mountains in Flagstaff, to the valley floor of Phoenix where the towering Saguaro Cacti thrive, and Red Rock country in between, Arizona is a fascinating state to travel. It is also perfectly situated to get to other interesting western destinations, many of which are dog friendly. One of our first trips with Nigel and Divot after the move was to southern California to visit friends. Our friends' well-mannered dogs, with their friendly acceptance of visitors and their gentle play, allowed Nigel to have even more positive experiences with other dogs. He was learning that not all dogs were obnoxious. Nigel was discovering that the company of other dogs could actually be enjoyable!

Nigel and Divot beat the Arizona summer heat by visiting Telluride, CO.

Our favorite spot to visit with Nigel and Divot was Telluride Mountain Village, a laid back picturesque ski-village surrounded by the majestic snow-covered Colorado Rockies. Telluride is very dog friendly and there are people with dogs everywhere. The village square is perfect for admiring the surrounding natural beauty, shopping, and people watching. Our favorite little outdoor eatery is located in the square, and Nigel and Divot were always welcome to sit under our table while we had a meal and enjoyed the views. This allowed them the opportunity to rest from the day's activities, and to also attract admirers.

Nigel, always outgoing with people and never one to shy away from shamelessly trying to capture someone's attention, preferred to be in the mix, not sitting under the table. We would attach his leash to one of the chairs so he could see every passerby, hoping to capture someone's attention. When eye contact was made, his wagging body and eager expression made the formal invitation. The majority of people who saw him would stop and pet him and some even took his picture or wanted their picture taken with him. Most would then strike up a conversation with us. A happy, friendly dog is the perfect way to bring down barriers and meet people.

Nigel works the crowd at Telluride Mountain Village.

That was all fine and well for Nigel, but for Divot it was all about relaxation. The sun always made Divot relaxed and drowsy, and as she preferred sitting on my lap to sitting under the table, she would adjust herself into the crook of my arm on her back, belly exposed, and fall asleep in the warm mountain sun. Let Nigel work the crowd, this was *her* vacation and she was going to catch up on her sleep. The sight of Divot lying on her back sunning herself, sometimes with mouth slightly agape, attracted as much attention as Nigel's overt efforts. Between the two of them they were a force to be reckoned with, daring anyone to ignore them.

With my hand to protect her tender belly, Divot has not a care in the world as she soaks up the sun in Telluride, CO.

Nigel and Divot turned out to be amazing little trail dogs! Often we would unleash them and other than a few "stop-and-sniffs" every so often, they followed right behind me or stayed beside me. We always hiked in tandem, so one of us walked in front of the dogs and one behind them. It was as if we had been doing this since puppyhood. All of our training efforts had paid off – we were taking our dogs everywhere and having a great time with them, doing things that a few short years before, seemed impossible. With all of us doing our part, we had reformed our homebody Nigel into a seasoned traveler!

~Teachable Moment~
Traveling with your dog.

Over the years we have had some fantastic times traveling with Nigel and Divot. Sure, it is not as easy as traveling with just humans, as you are limited in some of your activities, but it certainly can be fun. If your dogs are friendly like mine, you have many opportunities to meet interesting people. If you are uncomfortable kenneling your dog, or do not have a reliable friend or family member who can care for him, sometimes packing him up and taking him with you is your best bet. First, there are some things you should consider about traveling with your dog: 1) Your dog's health, 2) your dog's temperament, 3) your trip plans.

Health & Temperament
If your dog is in good health, there is probably no reason why he or she cannot safely travel with you. If your dog has ailments that cause him pain or discomfort, or he gets motion sickness, he will probably not be a good candidate for travel. If your dog is healthy, has an easy-going temperament, and is already well socialized, he will most likely travel well. If you are trying to reform a homebody like I did, you have much work to do *before* taking a vacation with him.

Trip Plans – Where Are You Going?

When traveling with a dog you will need to put more research into your travel plans then you might otherwise have to. Make sure that your dog is permitted in the places you want to visit, and make sure he is safe doing the activities you want to do. For example, many National Parks have only a few specific hiking trails that permit dogs, while others will limit your dog to the parking lot only. This is to protect the park's wildlife as well as your pet. Be sure you are aware of any potential health risks that exist in the area you are visiting.

Travel by car – things you will need for your dog:

- Travel crate or safety seat.
- Leash & collar with tags that include cell phone number and microchip information.
- Extra food. Always bring more than you will need in case of delay.
- Bottled water.
- Bowls for food and water.
- Medications and/or supplements.
- Treats and toys. Bully sticks or a stuffed Kong will help to work out any anxiety or boredom your dog may have.
- Pet toothbrush & paste.
- Brush.
- Roll of paper towels.
- Large towel – great for wet weather days.
- Waste bags.
- Large and small zip bags.
- Tick remover.
- Window screens for warm weather travel.

- Before heading out, do an Internet search of vets and E-vets in the areas through which you will be traveling and keep the information handy.
- I suggest avoiding the "pet area" at rest stops. It is a place where your dog can easily pick up intestinal parasites from heavy dog traffic.

Before heading out for a long trip, it is a good idea to take your dog for a walk to make sure he gets the chance to eliminate and burn off some excess energy. I have never been one to leave my dogs in the car while I go in to a restaurant to eat. When heading toward our destination, we eat food we have packed, or get take out food and eat in the vehicle, or find a pleasant place to picnic.

Travel by Plane

If you are flying with your pet, make reservations early, as there are only a limited number of animals allowed on a plane per seating class. Also consider the weather and time of year you are flying. In addition to the essentials of food, waste-pick up bags, etc., here are some other things you will need. (Items such as bottled water, roll of paper towels, and window screens will obviously not be taken on a flight.)

- Airline approved travel bag. Leave plenty of time to get your dog acclimated to it before your trip. Put an absorbent piddle pad inside the carrier just in case.
- Most airlines allow a maximum of 15 pounds for dog and travel bag combined. Check your airlines' travel policy for details
- Health certificate from your vet. Most airlines require that it be dated within 10 days of your departure. Check your airlines' policies for details.

- Gallon zipper bag (tuck in pocket of your dog's travel bag – see below).

Just the same as you would for car travel, take your dog for a brisk walk before heading to the airport so he can eliminate and get rid of excess energy. If possible, let him relieve himself one more time once at the airport. When you arrive at the airport have your health certificate ready to show the representative. When going through security you will carry your dog through the metal detector while his carrier goes through X-ray.

Once on board if your dog seems nervous, do nothing that would approve or encourage it. Give him the Kong you brought. (Save the bully stick for later. You don't want a potential choking incident at 35,000 feet.) Having something to do will occupy his mind and help with any anxiety.

Regarding the gallon zipper bag… On a trip back from California to Michigan with Divot, it seemed rather warm in the terminal and I was concerned that she would be even more uncomfortable once on the plane. I went to the nearest bar (where charming Divot, with her head poking out of her travel bag, was an instant hit with the patrons), and asked the kindly bartender if she could fill my gallon zipper bag with ice, which she did. I then tucked the bag of ice into the end pocket of Divot's carrier and the ice radiated coolness into her travel bag, keeping her cool and comfortable for the rest of the trip.

Having been properly acclimated to her new travel bag, Divot sits on the open flap. Clearly, she's ready for her trip!

Stay!

Pet friendly accommodations are becoming more common, and the choices range from budget to luxury. During our travels, we discovered that it is often the small boutique hotels that warmly welcome dogs, some offering baked dog cookies in the room upon check-in. While some places "accept pets" we choose the places that "warmly welcome pets," especially when staying for a few days. Upon entering the lobby of our hotel in Aspen, Colorado, we were greeted by a sign behind check-in desk that read, "NIGEL & DIVOT ARE IN THE HOUSE!" Now, *that's* the kind of place you will have fun staying with your dog! We also find that renting a private residence is a nice option when traveling with your dogs. It allows you to have more room, often a yard, and certainly more privacy for those late night and early morning potty outings. It goes without saying, please be a good ambassador for dog lovers everywhere; pick up after your dog, do not allow him to bother other guests, and do not leave your dog unattended in a hotel room. Please adhere to your hotel's and host's pet policies!

"Petiquette"

Whether you are on vacation or simply enjoying an afternoon out locally with your dog, please be considerate of other people. I call this "petiquette," or practicing proper etiquette when out with your dog. Not everyone loves dogs, or even likes them. Some people have allergies, and some people have a fear of dogs. No matter the situation, you must be aware of what your dog is doing always, and if he is behaving improperly, you must remove him from the situation.

If you will be dining out with your dog, feed him something first! When we first began to frequent outdoor eateries with Nigel and Divot, we found that it was difficult for them to sit patiently under a table when there was food all around and they were hungry but being forced to wait. After a multi-mile hike, they too had worked up an appetite and we learned to bring a meal for them to eat *before* we sat down to eat. Be sure to allow your dog time to eliminate before you arrive at the restaurant. A full tummy after a hike always gave Nigel and Divot good reason to be content to sit, or even nap under the table in the cool shade. Be sure you bring a water dish and water for your dog.

Traveling with your dog can be a rewarding, fun bonding experience. Because you will be in unfamiliar surroundings and it is likely you will be together constantly, you will need to be prepared for anything. Bring patience and creativity, and fond memories lie ahead. Don't forget your camera!

A NORWICH TALE
Just Drop It Will You? – September 2005
Really, who's training who?

It is wise to make sure your dog knows the "drop it" command. Divot, ever eager to please caught on to this command easily. On the other hand, though a highly intelligent dog, Nigel never seemed to connect the dots with this particular one. Perhaps it was not a question of catching on, but more that he did not *want* to. Maybe he figured that he had worked hard for whatever it was that he picked up, and giving it up was not in his plan. Several weeks ago however, the importance of obeying this command became very real, when I had to struggle to remove part of a golf tee from Nigel's mouth. Over the years, I have removed things from his mouth that are gross, such as discarded gum, and once I wrestled him for a decomposing toad (a match which I unfortunately lost, much to my later dismay as the toad went through the digestive process), but the pointed end of a golf tee is truly dangerous.

Clever Nigel has this training thing all figured out!

After the golf tee incident, I decided that the "drop it" command was top priority and we set to work on it immediately. As we prepared for our morning walk, I put a handful of his favorite venison jerky treats in my pocket and we headed out. Near the end of our walk, Nigel picked up a small stick and I seized the opportunity to shove treats under his nose as I firmly said, "Drop it!" He dropped the stick and chose the treats. I lavished praise upon him and he seemed to be very proud of himself, and quite pleased with the trade we had just made. The next day, as fate would have it, he picked up another small stick and again, I firmly said, "Drop it" and put the treats under his nose. As I had hoped, he dropped the stick and took the treats.

Nigel is a very smart dog and when I figure out how to properly convey my thoughts to him, he catches on quickly, but nevertheless I was still surprised at just how quickly he was catching on. Days went by, and our daily walks allowed us to practice the new command, the outcome always being success. One morning as we walked along, Nigel picked up a clump of cut grass and dropped it as I gave the command. It all happened so fast that I had not quite gotten the command out when he dropped the clump of grass. He actually dropped it a little too fast but I gave him a treat and praised him. On a walk the same evening, he picked up a stone and dropped it immediately. He stood looking up at me, quite pleased with himself. It was then I realized that not only had he caught on to the command but had gone beyond it. He was now picking up objects that he could drop for me, to get the treat. The tables had turned – he was now training me. ^..^

A NORWICH TALE
You Want A Piece of Me? – April 2006

Fearless little Divot does not always understand the reality of the situation.

Living with a Norwich Terrier can sometimes seem like you are living with two different dogs in one. Divot is the sweetest, cuddliest, most lovable little dog ever. She is also quiet, submissive and easy going. That is when she is with humans. The other side of Divot is the fearless terrier side – she is a tough and mighty huntress with the heart of a lion! Or does a lion have the heart of a terrier?

One recent evening around dusk Mike went out to the patio with the dogs while I was finishing up in the office, planning to join them momentarily. A few minutes had passed when suddenly Mike knocked on the office window and pointed back toward the patio as he ran by. He was heading toward the neighbor's house, which was still under construction. When I reached the patio door, Nigel was standing at the door, and Mike yelled back at me, "Get him inside!" Nigel ran inside the house, not even needing to be coaxed. If you know anything about Nigel by now, you know that he is not only brilliant but he is somewhat cowardly. He will at all costs, remove himself from any danger – real or imagined. As Nigel scooted in, I ran outside to see that Mike had just scooped up Divot who had been nose to nose with a javelina, and thankfully a fence separated them.

It was a fence, but it was a view fence that a javelina snout, or a Norwich muzzle could easily fit through. Divot's body was rigid and the fur on her back was standing up straight. She was ready to rumble. Even though she was being swiftly carried away, she did not seem to feel it and she remained rigid, but still trying to look back at the wild beast. I put her in the house with Nigel who was watching the whole scene from his safe place, and once inside, she threw a fit. She was barking and pawing at the door – she had seen the javelina first and it was *her* prize! If she could speak I imagined it would be something like, *"You want a piece of me piggy? Bring it!"*

We stood watching this unusual animal for a few minutes, and left to his own, he eventually found his way back to where he came from. While the story might seem strange to some who do not have wild pig-like animals roaming through their neighborhoods, the larger point is that these little terriers, (apparently except for Nigel) are fearless, and it is this terrier trait that can get them into trouble as their instincts take over and reality takes a back seat. ^..^

Chapter 11

Scorpions, and Tarantulas, and Cacti! Oh My!

INTO THE VALLEY OF THE SUN

After a few years in the high desert of Sedona, though the beauty was unique and special, we realized it was too far away from some things that we wanted better access to such as the airport, veterinary services, and other things that make day-to-day life more convenient. In spring of 2007, we relocated to Phoenix – the Valley of the Sun.

To say that Phoenix summers are hot is an understatement of epic proportions. While we certainly enjoyed the dry, sometimes fierce heat, summers were hard on Nigel and Divot. Walks were done early in the morning – by 4:30 a.m. if we wanted to beat the heat. Not that overnight temperatures of 95° weren't *hot* but factor in the sun and your morning stroll gets terribly uncomfortable to say the least. Still, at 4:30 in the morning we saw many of our neighbors, also dedicated dog lovers, out walking their dogs too. At dawn, the sun's glow would begin to spread over the desert landscape, blanketing everything in its path, in brilliant orange. This glow provided the perfect backlight for the giant Saguaro Cacti that stood like sentries guarding our neighborhood. As daylight took over, a strange exchange took place as we humans came out to begin our day, and the desert predators receded back into their dens to escape the heat. It was not unusual to see coyotes and bobcats scurrying home after a night of hunting. Once back from our morning walk, most of Nigel and Divot's summer days were spent inside the house. At least twice each summer we would pack up and head to the mountains for cooler temperatures and some adventure, reinvigorating Nigel and Divot once again!

A NORWICH TALE

Irritable Bowl Syndrome– March 2007

Nigel defeats a mealtime foe.

For a while now I have been hearing about potential dangers found in some imported pet products. Concerns have been raised about products such as toys and dishes, but most recently, deadly ingredients have been discovered in some pet foods. I had always used ceramic dishes for Nigel and Divot, but as the evidence continued to mount, I decided to replace their food and water bowls with stainless steel. I bought sturdy bowls with non-slip bottoms, as Nigel and Divot tend to show a great deal of enthusiasm when it comes to eating.

Nigel does not always readily adapt to change, but I was quite surprised at his reaction to the new bowls. When dinnertime came, I put the food in their dishes and gave Nigel and Divot the "okay" to come and eat. Divot began to eat her food with her usual enthusiasm, but Nigel did not. As he lowered his head to the bowl, he stopped and backed up quickly. He tilted his head from side to side as Norwich do (yet another charming trait) when they are either listening or trying to understand something. He approached his bowl again but then, he backed up and barked at it! At first I could not understand what the problem could be. I knelt near his bowl and en-couraged him to eat some of the food from my hand, which he readily did, but when I backed away, he did too. Frustrated, he barked at the bowl again and tried to paw at it – from a safe distance of course. As I again returned my hand to his bowl, I realized what the problem was. He could see his reflection in the bowl!

By now, Divot had finished her food and was eyeing Nigel's unclaimed dish, so I took her out of the room and then came back to encourage Nigel. He so desperately wanted his food but the "intruder" in his bowl was upsetting him, and making mealtime – his favorite time – very uncomfortable! Eventually his empty tummy won out and he boldly approached the bowl and ate his food. He had a little difficulty when the pesky intruder again showed up in the water bowl, but with a little encouragement from me and from Divot, he overcame that too. ^..^

A NORWICH TALE

The Bully – July 2007

Is the bully the chew stick or the cute little girl dog?

Nigel and Divot have always had good things to chew on, such as bully sticks. They love these chews and they get very excited when I get the bullies out and start making preparations for giving them one. The preparation is spreading out a large old towel to cover the carpet in my office. This ancient towel with its faded beach motif is referred to as "the Binky." Once the floor is properly covered, I go to the kitchen to get the bully sticks, and while I'm doing that Nigel and Divot each choose their spot on the Binky and wait for my return. Once bullies are handed out, they each go to their own end of the Binky to enjoy their chew. As is Divot's custom now, she begins to chew enthusiastically on her stick, but this lasts for only a few minutes because she has suddenly realized that the stick she *really* wanted, was the one that I just gave to Nigel.

The reality is that it would not matter which stick Divot got – she always wants the *other* one. I can't take Nigel's stick away from him to give to her because that wouldn't be fair. So, Divot sets her sights on waiting him out. She sits as close to him as possible while staring at me, imploring me to take it away from him. She will occasionally let out a little whimper or a grunt hoping this will have an affect on either Nigel or me. It has no effect on Nigel, who continues to happily chew, ignoring her grunts, whimpers, and occasional squeaks. I think she is adorable and it is very hard to not help her and give her what she wants. She continues her vigil for the bully stick – the one she knows was *truly* meant for her.

After Nigel has had a good, long chew on the bully stick, I suggest a carrot, and he drops the bully stick and follows me to the kitchen. Divot, thrilled with this new turn of events, picks up the discarded bully stick and has her turn at it. Sometimes Nigel will pick up her unwanted stick but often, he's just had enough and he goes on to the next activity, which is usually a nap. This is the way things normally go but several days ago, Divot realized that she was missing out on something, and this smart, sassy little terrier set about rectifying the situation.

"I really don't see why I can't have that one." Nigel and Divot on the Binky. *Is "the bully" the chewing stick or is the bully the cute little girl dog?*

When the time came for the carrot switch, Nigel and I headed to the kitchen as usual. As I was feeding him pieces of carrot, Divot suddenly came running into the kitchen with the big bully stick still in her mouth, which made for quite an amusing sight. With lightening speed she dropped the bully stick, gulped a piece of carrot, picked up the stick, and ran back toward my office with the bully stick in her mouth. Just as suddenly as she ran off, she returned (the bully stick still in her mouth), and headed toward that patio door throwing me a look that said, "Out please!" I opened the door and out she went. She relieved herself (bully stick still in her mouth), and came bounding through the door and returned to my office to the Binky. Apparently this bully stick was just too good to put down, even with nature calling! ^..^

AWAKENING TO A NIGHTMARE

When I walked into the living room where Nigel was lounging in his bed one afternoon in mid February of 2008, I saw that he was awake, but noticed that his right eye was closed. I observed him for a few moments and realized that he was definitely keeping the right eye closed, while the left eye remained open. I said, "Hey Nigel?" He opened the right eye and looked at me as if to say, "Hmm?" This behavior continued on and off for a while, and thinking perhaps he had gotten something in his eye, I took him to the vet to have the eye examined. The vet found nothing in the eye, but during the exam he noted that the gum area around one of Nigel's premolars on the right side looked irritated, and thought that perhaps the closed eye was a reaction to possible tooth pain. He recommended that we have Nigel's teeth checked and cleaned, so an appointment was scheduled for two days later.

Fortunate to have good teeth his whole life, at 10 years of age, this was only the second time Nigel had needed to have his teeth cleaned. Still very fearful at the vet, he was highly agitated when we checked in for his appointment. I asked if the vet could give him something to calm down right away, and I was assured that he would. Several hours later I received a phone call saying that Nigel had done well and was resting. The suspicious tooth and surrounding gum area had been checked and while needing a little cleaning, were found to be in good condition, but another, smaller bottom tooth had been extracted. I was relieved that everything had gone well, but that good feeling did not last long. I picked Nigel up later that afternoon, and from the time I brought him home, I could see that something was wrong. His left front paw was dragging and he remained highly agitated. I knew he was probably hungry but there was just something odd about his behavior.

When I called to express my concern, the person at the vet's office suggested that the dragging paw and the agitation was probably from the effects of the pain medication he had been given. Additionally, he had been given an antibiotic. It took Nigel several more hours to calm down, even a little. Some food helped but, still, he did not seem to be comfortable, mentally or physically. There was just *something* about him. By the following day his weaker, dragging paw had not corrected itself and I reported this to the vet. In our conversation I expressed concern about a possible stroke. Why would a perfectly healthy and robust dog go in for teeth cleaning and come out dragging his paw? The vet assured me that strokes in dogs are rare, and he was doubtful that Nigel had suffered a stroke. Still he had no explanation for the dragging paw. I asked, "Could his blood pressure have been too high when he was anesthetized? Could that have done something neurologically?" Again, I was assured that it would have no effect. Still I had doubts.

Another day passed and Nigel was becoming more uncoordinated. On our morning walk, he wanted to run but when attempting to jump up on a curb – something he did every day – he stumbled, his chest hitting the curb with a thud. He could run normally, but his fine motor skills were lacking. Later that evening as we were settled in watching TV, Mike said, "Honey come here and feel Nigel's head. Is his *head* caved in?" Much to my horror, as I felt the right side of his head, that is exactly what it felt like, though he showed no pain or discomfort when we touched his head. After a sleepless night, first thing the next morning I was back at the vet when they opened, asking what this was all about. The vet's response was, "It feels like the muscles there have atrophied." When pressed why this would suddenly happen on one side of his head, he looked perplexed and had no answer. I explained the issue of what seemed to be fine motor skill impairment, but because Nigel was so agitated at the vet's office, it was hard for the vet to see what we were seeing at home. I went home frustrated, and started my research. I needed more information and another opinion. Besides the dragging paw issue, when I handed out bully sticks that afternoon, Nigel seemed a bit confused and was not coordinated enough to hold his stick between his paws – something that comes natural to any dog. My concern growing, I got out my video camera. I had to prove that there were problems. The next morning I awoke to a nightmare...

It was as if Nigel had become both geriatric and senile over night. He stumbled and bumped into walls and furniture, and sometimes even when sitting down he toppled over. When standing still his body swayed, and when walking down the long hallway, he pressed against the left wall rather than walking down the middle as he usually did. When in an open room, he tried to seek out a wall to guide him, always pressing toward his left. Outside, with open space around him, he seemed frightened and confused. Mostly, he had a terrible vacant look in his eyes. It was too early for the vet to be open but I knew I would be there when the doors opened. As I was getting ready, I filmed his strange behaviors, but it was only then, when I watched Nigel through the camera's eye did I notice yet another problem – when not able to press against a wall, he was walking in tight circles. My heart sank.

The vet confirmed that something neurological was indeed wrong, and by now no video was needed. Nigel paced around the small exam room, clinging tightly to the wall, and when moved away from the wall he walked in tight circles. Some preliminary neurological tests were done, to which Nigel's responses seemed very slow and deficient, and it appeared that he had lost the vision in his left eye. Initially the term "vestibular disease" was mentioned, but his symptoms combined with the change in his skull shape added to the concern. The vet scheduled the first available appointment with a veterinary neurologist for the following morning. I called Mike, who was away on a business trip, and told him what was happening. He headed home immediately. For the rest of the day, Nigel paced aimlessly hardly stopping, and when he did stop, he walked in tight circles. When Mike arrived home later that day he was shocked and horrified to see how Nigel's condition had deteriorated. Throughout the rest of the night, poor Nigel paced endlessly.

The next morning we met with the neurologist. An MRI showed a small mass at the base of Nigel's brain. Equally of immediate concern, was a large amount of swelling around the mass, nearly four times the size of the actual mass. This was concentrated on the right side of his skull. There was no way to know what had caused the swelling, but immediate action needed to be taken to bring it down. Since the swelling and thus the pressure were on the right side of his brain, the left side of his body was affected. If the mass was benign, and the swelling came down, there was no reason to think that Nigel would not live a normal life, but if it were cancerous, there would be no hope. Surgery was not an option. If it was cancerous we would know soon enough as Nigel might improve initially when the swelling came down, but it would only be a brief respite; the symptoms would return, and as the vet said, *"If he doesn't get better, then we're going to know."*

Nigel receives "Get Well" wishes from an old friend in Michigan.

Nigel was put on a steroid, an antibiotic, and even though he tested negative for it, he was put on an anti-fungal medication for treatment of possible Coccidioidomycosis, commonly known as valley fever. Valley fever is caused by the fungus "Coccidioides immitis" that is found in the soil of Southwestern deserts. It is noteworthy that valley fever not only affects dogs, but it can also affect people. One of our breeders had told us about valley fever before we left Michigan but I had no idea how prevalent a problem it was. Valley fever usually affects a dog's respiratory system, but if the infection spreads outside the lungs it can cause a larger, more systemic problem – disseminated valley fever. Symptoms of valley fever include: lack of energy, coughing, fever, and loss of appetite. Disseminated valley fever can cause seizures, cause sores to erupt on the skin, cause back and neck pain, and even render a dog lame.

From the time we arrived in Phoenix, both dogs had been tested for valley fever as part of their annual checkups, and both had always tested negative. Since there was little to go on, and no clear explanation for the swelling in Nigel's head, we were willing to try anything. We brought Nigel home and waited. By early evening, he finally rested, even dreaming a little as he slept. The quiet of the evening was punctuated with the soft sound of "yip, yip, yip" as he dreamt. Nigel's little legs were able to run strong and fast in his dreamscape. This was the first sign of normalcy I had seen in several days.

For the first few days after his MRI and beginning of treatment, Nigel was very weak and unsteady. Having been a strong, independent, and hardy dog his entire life, we were not used to seeing him so weak and vulnerable. Even when Nigel was having difficulty with his balance and would occasionally topple over, Divot was never short with him, nor did she ever nip at him. Instead she stayed near him. Without Nigel by her side, at first Divot refused to go for walks.

Over the next few weeks Nigel continued to gain strength and began showing significant progress. His head returned to its normal shape, and the sight returned in his left eye. By mid March we were able to lower some of his medication dosages. Still, his left front paw continued to drag. From the time of the dental visit, the paw was never the same, and no answer for it has been forthcoming even all these years later. I pushed the vet for some logical reason behind it but he had nothing to offer. I asked the neurologist about a possible stroke and he said that no indication of a stroke was found on the MRI. Nigel continued to make slow and steady progress, and we began to feel confident that the mass was benign. The neurologist wanted to repeat the MRI to see if there had been any change but we declined, not wanting to anesthetize Nigel again, and frankly, if the mass was growing, there was nothing we could do about it.

Wanting to make sure that Divot had her exercise but not wanting to exclude Nigel, at first we carried him along on our morning walks and he seemed to enjoy seeing neighbors, and getting out in the fresh air. Eventually we got the okay for him to start with a short morning amble and he seemed quite pleased to join us on his own four feet again. As the months went by he began to regain his strength and vigor. By late September of 2008, he was doing so well, he was able to accompany us on a trip to Park City, UT where he even did some light hiking. At 10 years of age, this tough little terrier was still going strong!

Divot and Nigel pose on a fallen log.
Hiking near Bald Mountain near Park City, UT.

~Teachable Moment~
Do not take anesthesia lightly!

Anesthetizing our dogs has become commonplace in modern veterinary medicine. General anesthesia is of course needed for major surgeries, but it is also sometimes necessary for seemingly simple procedures such as having a dog X-rayed. And, since dogs cannot be asked to lie still and open wide, general anesthesia is necessary for having your dogs teeth cleaned. When your vet does any surgical procedure, it is highly unlikely that he or she will have a veterinary anesthesiologist to assist, so your vet will most likely be handling all critical aspects of the surgery including monitoring your pet. This does not mean that your dog will not be getting the best possible care from your veterinarian – that's just the way it is. That said, I do everything possible to avoid anesthesia for my dogs, such as brushing their teeth daily, feeding a healthy diet, and doing whatever I can to keep them healthy and fit. What happened to Nigel is proof that anesthesia is not to be taken lightly – there is always a risk! I am not blaming anyone for what happened to him. I certainly do wish that a better explanation had been forthcoming but I cannot change the past, I can only go forward with lessons learned.

A NORWICH TALE
A Tale of True Friendship – February 2008

A friend in need...

Divot's favorite spot in my office is on a blanket under my desk. Nigel usually chooses the dog bed or he sprawls out on the floor. When it's cold, they often share the dog bed, but very rarely do they lie actually touching each other. This "bubble" is Nigel's choice – he likes to be touched only when he feels like it. Sometimes if they are sharing the bed and he wants to snuggle, he will curl up and put his head on Divot. She never minds. Divot will snuggle with anyone.

The day after his MRI, when he was still very weak and wobbly, Nigel crawled under my desk, taking Divot's usual spot. Ordinarily such an act would result in her giving him "the look" (the look can also be accompanied by her squirrel chatter, or an impatient grunting sound), which always sends him running, tail tucked. But this day, Divot instead stood observing Nigel for a few minutes, apparently not giving him "the look," just observing him. Then, she carefully and gently crawled under the desk and lay next to him. She was so close to him that their heads were touching. It appeared from my human perspective that she was trying to comfort him. Equally surprising, Nigel did not get up and leave as he normally would. Instead he stayed where he was, dozing on and off, as if he was comforted by her closeness. Surprised by his willingness to be touched and even apparently comforted by her, I got out the camera and snapped photo after photo of them, capturing this very unique and tender moment.

A friend indeed. Divot snuggles with Nigel the day after his MRI.

I have always wondered what happened between the two of them that day. What silent information was exchanged? Were Divot's actions a true attempt to offer him comfort? I will never know for sure what happened, but I think that I witnessed something very special between two pack mates. ^..^

FEELING DOWN IN THE VALLEY

After Nigel had made such a stunning recovery from his illness, we were concerned when in December of the following year, he began to slow down on our morning walks. He was still raring to go, sitting expectantly at the front door with Divot as always, but once out, he seemed void of his usual energy. We attributed it to age finally slowing him down, after all, Divot did not have the speed and stamina that she once did either. Our once brisk morning walks were now slow morning strolls but the change of pace was fine with us. One evening as he slept on the sofa between us, we noticed that Nigel's breathing seemed unusually rapid, and quite shallow. I took him to the vet the following day to have him examined. He was given a general exam, blood was drawn, and his temperature was taken. It was elevated to 104.5°. Also during the general exam, Nigel showed sensitivity to touch, especially on his back, so in addition, X-rays were done. The X-rays showed no back problems, but did show inflammation in his right lung. He was given an antibiotic and a steroid and, since valley fever is ever a possibility in Phoenix, he was given an anti-fungal medication again. A few days later his blood work came back and everything looked normal except his valley fever test, which was borderline, but not definitive. We decided to keep him on the anti-fungal and retest him again in three weeks. Over the next two weeks he got a little better and then worse, then a little better, then worse. Sometimes we would count his resting breathing rate in the 80 beats per minute range. It was frightening.

Though he had stopped showing interest in walks, when his always hardy appetite diminished, I took him back for another valley fever test, a week earlier than planned. Another chest X-ray was done. The inflammation had gotten much worse and his temperature had risen to 105.4°. When the blood test came back it was positive – he definitely had valley fever.

After Nigel's diagnosis, through discussions with our neighbors, we learned that roughly 75% of the people we knew either had a dog that had contracted valley fever or knew of someone's dog that did. This news was stunning and would be part of our consideration to leave desert life a few years later.

With medication and plenty of rest, over the next three months, our hardy little Nigel regained his strength. Our vet was very impressed at the strength this now 11-year old had. At his 90-day check up, his valley fever test came back negative – he had beaten it! One day later, feeling *so* good he jumped up, excited about a stuffed Kong I was carrying, and tore the ACL (Anterior Cruciate Ligament) in his left rear leg. Because his bout with valley fever had weakened his immune system, he was not a good candidate for corrective surgery. He was put on pain medication, and limited activity, at least for a while. We were told that he was not permitted to jump anymore. His days jumping up on the furniture, sleeping on the bed with us, and most sadly, his days of hiking were over. With his left front paw already in a permanently weakened state and now the left rear leg damaged, we were unsure about what his quality of life would be.

A NORWICH TALE
Coach Nigel – July 2008

Never underestimate the benefits of a dog who loves a routine!

Both Nigel and Divot love a routine. Sure they'll put up with us if we deviate from the norm, but the act of deviation is not without question on their part, especially Nigel. With Phoenix weather swings, hot mornings in summer and cold, often windy mornings in the winter, I still rely on my treadmill for walking or running in comfort. Every morning after one cup of coffee, I get up and prepare to "hit the mill" as I call it. When I start to make these preparations, Nigel and Divot are on my heels. They follow me to the bedroom and patiently wait while I change into my workout clothes. Then we're off to the kitchen to fill my water bottle, followed by a quick trip to my office to get my iPod, and check e-mail. They are always right behind me, following me from room to room, observing each activity. Some mornings though, I am disorganized and I backtrack and return to the bedroom or to my office several times. Tired of following me back and forth, Divot heads to the workout room to get a head start on her nap. Though he has stopped following me too, Nigel chooses to sit at the intersection of my paths, still able to keep an eye on me but no longer interested in putting the energy into following me around. After all, it's supposed to be *my* workout, not his.

With all the preparations done, we are now off to the workout room. Sometimes however, as I am prone to do on those disorganized mornings, I make a trip or two in and out of the workout room. And just when it looked like I was getting it together! It is at this point that Coach Nigel lets me know that if I plan to skip the workout, it will not be without great disappointment on his part. He sits next to the treadmill, looking at me expectantly. As I finally do get my act together, and board the treadmill, he takes his place lying next to it, usually with his back pressed up against the side. I do not know what causes him to have such dedication to my workouts, but after just a few minutes, both he and Divot are sleeping peacefully as I start to break a sweat.

When I am finished and slow the treadmill speed, they both wake up stretching and yawning and then head for the kitchen. What's next? See what I'm having for breakfast of course! ^..^

A NORWICH TALE

Popcorn! – August 2009

Please, just one more piece!

Yesterday evening, I had an appointment and I returned home too late to make a proper dinner for myself. Feeling somewhat lazy and uninspired to cook anything, I decided that a bowl of popcorn would be perfect for dinner. When it comes to popcorn, Nigel and Divot go crazy. It is the only food that makes them drool. After popping, I take some out, and set it aside for them, after carefully removing the hulls. I finished my "dinner" and put the bowl with the leftover popcorn on the kitchen island and we all settled in for the evening. Later, as we prepared for bed, Mike took Nigel and Divot out for their final potty break and I prepared the coffee maker for the morning. As I did my preparations I picked out a few kernels of the leftover popcorn to munch on. Just as I put a piece into my mouth, Nigel and Divot came bounding in the door, and saw me snacking. Of course they each wanted a piece, so they had one and off to bed we went.

Who could deny Divot anything?

Usually when I put Divot on our bed, she immediately starts the nesting process on the blankets or my pillow – whichever place she had decided to hunker down – but this particular evening rather than her usual routine, she sat on the edge of the bed looking expectantly at me. As I dried my face, I noticed that she was still sitting on the edge of the bed. I said, "Divie, do you need to go potty again?" She showed no reaction. Again I said, "Divie, do you need to go *potty*?" Again, no reaction. Next I tried, "Divie, do you need a *drink*?" Still nothing. So, placing her on the floor I said, "Okay, show me." As she happily trotted down the hallway, she looked back several times to make sure I was still following her. She took me right to the kitchen island and stood at the spot where the popcorn bowl was, her little tail wagging excitedly, with a look on her face that said, *"That's what I want! I want more popcorn!"* I said, "You want some *popcorn*?" She did one of her pop and spin moves, clearly indicating that I had guessed correctly. I could not believe that she had pieced all of this together. It was genius! I picked her up, gave her a piece of popcorn and said, "Happy now?"

She replied with her usual lick on my cheek and off to bed we went where she settled down immediately and went to sleep. ^..^

A NORWICH TALE

I Can Do That Too! – October 2009

Perhaps "manipulative" should be in the breed standard.

After we arrived in Arizona in 2005, Divot developed a dangerous new behavior of eating stones. This behavior, called pica – meaning eating things that aren't food – can signal the development of a compulsive disorder, or possibly indicate the lack of a particular nutrient in an adult dog. Opinions vary on the reasons why some dogs develop these abnormal cravings. While this behavior is something that curious puppies sometimes do, it is disturbing when your adult dog starts such a behavior. On our cross-country move from Michigan to Arizona, Divot had contracted Giardia, an intestinal parasite. The presence of this hard to detect parasite made her terribly sick, and I believe that the illness was the root cause of the new behavior of stone eating. Eating objects such as stones can be dangerous – even deadly – so when it began, I gave her nutritional supplements, but also started to work with her to stop the behavior. Thankfully, she moved beyond it but it took nearly two years.

There have been occasional lapses when she will still pick up a stone, but, being a people pleaser, she immediately drops it when given the command, even without the offer of a treat. As you may have read in an older tale, I taught Nigel the same command when he picked up a golf tee one morning. He took to the training right away and almost immediately began to manipulate me by picking up things and dropping them just to get a treat.

Just a few days ago, Nigel picked up something from the sidewalk. I immediately gave him the "drop it" command and he did immediately drop the object, and then of course looked expectantly for the treat that was owed him. I checked my jacket pocket and found a forgotten piece of kibble and gave it to him as I praised him.

Never one to be left out of any praise (or any treats for that matter), Divot almost immediately picked up a pebble and dropped it – even without the command! She was wagging her little tail, looking quite proud of herself. But, I had nothing in my pocket! I squatted down to pet her, and praised her for dropping the pebble and we continued on. Again, she picked up a pebble and dropped it. She was so adorable, and so pleased with herself! Digging around in my pocket, hoping to find an overlooked piece of kibble and finding none, I again offered her praise instead. As we walked on – or tried to – she continued to pick up pebbles and drop them, sometimes almost tossing them at me. She did not stop until I finally gathered some kibble dust from the bottom of my pocket and let her lick the dust off my finger. That seemed to satisfy her and we all walked on. A case in which something is better than nothing! ^..^

A NORWICH TALE

Going Bananas – January 2010

Nigel and Divot go ape for bananas!

Nigel and Divot have always loved bananas. No matter where they are in the house, when they hear the sound of a banana being broken off the bunch, they come running. It is truly amazing how good their hearing is when it comes to food.

Nigel and Divot are used to going places with us, especially on the weekends, and last Saturday was no different. We were heading out to run some errands and stopped at our local Starbucks to get our coffee. Most of the people who work there recognize us, or more likely they recognize our dogs. As we rounded the corner heading for the pickup window, we both saw what was ahead. At the same time, we both said, "See that?" There at the pickup window was a pretty basket, and in the basket? Apples and bananas! As we pulled up and stopped at the window, Nigel spotted the bananas and his nose went into the air. He immediately began to whine, whimper, and lick his chops. Divot, in her seat on the other side of the vehicle, joined in, not quite sure what all the excitement was about, but definitely not wanting to be left out of anything.

Seeing their excitement, the young man at the window made a big fuss over them and thought that all the excitement was about seeing him. We didn't have the heart to tell him that all the excitement was about seeing the bananas. We got our coffee and left still laughing about Nigel's "suburban hunting" skills.

Chapter 12
Sweet Carolina

HOME AGAIN

Mike and I often say that we are bona fide homebodies but you would never know it by our frequent relocations for work as of late, but home truly is our favorite place to be. Home is anywhere we are with Nigel and Divot, and Nigel and Divot make any place home sweet home.

In the summer of 2010 Mike was offered a job in Charlotte, North Carolina. Not excited about going through a move again, but grateful for a good opportunity, we decided to take the chance. We had six weeks to move and settle in before Mike was to start his new job. We found a lovely place with a big yard – perfect for Nigel and Divot! The neighborhood felt very reminiscent of our Michigan neighborhood that we loved so much. It was like going home again. We were happy that Nigel and Divot's golden years would be spent in this beautiful spot with green grass, pretty flowers, and an abundance of squirrels to chase. While we loved the dry desert climate, admittedly, after Nigel's bout with valley fever, some of the shine had worn off the desert for us. We were concerned that he would get sick again and that Divot might get it too. We saw the move as the best thing for all of us. Being seasoned movers, we began to plan and pack for our move, and I told Nigel and Divot, "This is it Little Ones – our last move. I promise!"

EIGHT DAYS

We were in the process of finishing the plans for our relocation with only eight days to go before moving day. We were feeling that we had accomplished a lot in a short time and felt positive about our progress. I was tying up loose ends with my home watch business on the morning of July 28, 2010, when I received a call from Mike. He said, "You have to get home now! Something has happened to Divot. I think she had a seizure. Hurry!" I flew out the door, and as I drove home, my mind churned, *"A seizure? No, he's wrong. She's 12 years old – she has never had a seizure. This can't be happening. Oh please no! This can't be happening. Hang on Divie – I'm coming home!"* I arrived a few minutes later to find Mike sitting on the living room floor with her. He did not look well. By this time however, Divot was on her feet and came toward me. She was a little unsteady, and weak on her left side, but she came to me. I scooped her up and held her close while Mike relayed the story of what happened...

"She was sleeping soundly in my office so I left her there and I came into the kitchen to make breakfast. A few minutes later, I heard a thumping sound, and I ran back to my office and found her on her side, thrashing around. It looked like she was trying to get up, but she couldn't get off her side. I could see that she was stiff but her front legs were paddling. When I picked her up, her face was all wet – she was drooling thick, foamy stuff. It was all over the floor and on her face."

I asked him if he had seen anything on the floor. With all the moving, could a poisonous spider have come out of hiding and bitten her? What about a scorpion sting? We never left any chemicals around and frankly, there was nothing in Mike's office or anywhere that she could have gotten into. It was just a few minutes after 7:00 a.m., but I called our vet anyway. I left a message with a few details and said I was on my way with Divot. We would be there when they opened at 7:30. Moments later, someone from the office called my cell phone and said to come right in – they would be watching for us.

As I drove the short seven minutes to the vet's office, Divot slept on the front seat of the car completely exhausted. I relayed Mike's story to the vet. During the exam Divot could hardly stand up or even stay awake. The vet gave her a thorough exam, took her vitals and took some blood. Her blood pressure and pulse were very low. He said that he was doubtful that it had been a sting or a bite. The usual reaction to either would not a seizure. He said that at her age sudden seizure onset could be the result of stress, head trauma, an organ malfunction, or it could be neurological in nature.

I tried to stay calm but this was almost more than I could bear. We were moving across the county in eight days and out of nowhere my sweet Divot has a *seizure*? I was confused and frightened. My heart ached. I knew that she had not suffered any head trauma – we both worked from home and we were with the dogs nearly 24 hours a day and had been for their entire lives. *Did we cause her stress with another move? We were only trying to do what was best for all of us. The new place was going to be perfect for them! Did she have a brain tumor? Oh please no, not that! What would I do if she had a seizure en route?* As the vet and I spoke, Divot slept soundly in my arms, exhausted from the ordeal. I held her close, trying to stay strong, and stay calm. A few days later, her blood tests came back. There was nothing found that gave any explanation for a seizure.

THE FALL OF OCTOBER

The cross-country move went without incident and we felt a tremendous relief when we arrived at our new home. With a variety of both deciduous and evergreen trees, and an abundance of lush green grass, the softness of the North Carolina landscape is the polar opposite of the hard, sometimes unforgiving Arizona desert. With the oppressive heat and humidity of summer gone now, the clear autumn sunlight seemed to set the brightly colored leaves ablaze. Surrounded by this familiar beauty, we felt comfortable right away.

While much slower these days, Nigel and Divot loved to amble around their big, new yard, and the cool autumn weather seemed to invigorate them. They adapted to their new surroundings quite well, enjoying a softer world again. "Adaptable" was a word I had always ascribed to Divot but now it was equally fitting for Nigel too. Nigel and Divot took short walks around the neighborhood with us, and met some of their new neighbors. Everyone immediately loved our friendly little terriers and we could not have been more pleased. It was so good to feel at home again!

Home again, home again.
Nigel & Divot at home in Charlotte, NC.

We enjoyed exploring our new home state and did some day trips with Nigel and Divot. Though they no longer had the energy for the rigorous hikes of their youth, at 12 years old, they still enjoyed gentle strolls through small towns with us, and if they got too tired, they were now content to be carried. The artistic community of Asheville embraces dogs as much as the art and cultural diversity it is known for, and it was one of our first destinations with Nigel and Divot. On another outing, we visited historic Old Salem on a particularly brisk fall morning. Both were so invigorated by the cool temperatures they wanted to run and pounce on blowing leaves!

It was another beautiful fall morning in early October, just two months after our move, when I was finishing a phone conversation with my Mother. Nigel and Divot were sleeping in their bed in the living room, just a few feet from me. Suddenly, Divot began to have a seizure. I hung up the phone and immediately looked at my watch. It was 11:56 a.m., October 4, 2010, – exactly 68 days after her first seizure. I began to make mental notes of what was happening: her entire body was rigid, she was drooling a lot of thick saliva, and her mouth was slightly open. Her eyes remained open and seemed vacant. I held Divot and spoke soothingly and calmly to her. The seizure abruptly ended with her shaking her head. Though the seizure lasted less than one minute, it seemed like an hour. After it was over, I continued to hold her and pet her, hoping to make her feel secure. Like after the first seizure, she was weaker on her left side, and she seemed confused. 15 minutes later, I carried her outside and she relieved herself. Once back inside, she slept for hours. As I thought about the preceding hours, I remembered that Divot shook her head several times that morning. It was unusual enough that I checked her ears but did not find any debris or detect an unusual scent. Also I remembered thinking that she had been a bit more clingy that morning. Suddenly I felt very isolated and very afraid. *Now what?*

The vet I had chosen was close by, less than three minutes away, which was convenient and somewhat comforting. The size of the small practice did concern me at first. In the event that we needed an appointment immediately, I was concerned that it might not be possible. But the office was spotlessly clean, and the vet had a comfortable way about her, and both

Nigel and Divot seemed to like her. I brought Divot to see her and she wanted to run the usual blood tests, but she was concerned that the seizures might be caused by a heart condition. *A heart condition?* We did a battery of tests on Divot, including an ultrasound on her heart and liver, but nothing definitive was found. Her liver bile acids were slightly elevated but again, not anything that pointed to seizures. Though the vet reported that the ultrasound revealed the beginning stages of mitral valve disease (MVD), it was still not a big enough concern to even warrant treatment. From the reading I had done, I understood that a heart condition might cause *fainting* but not seizures. Our new vet was also concerned about Divot's blood pressure, which she claimed was abnormally high, even though Divot did not fit the profile for hypertension. Despite my suggestion that the trauma she had just experienced, possibly coupled with "white coat syndrome" (a common condition in which some people and some animals have elevated blood pressure when seeing a doctor, or in the case of our dogs, a veterinarian), might be the cause of an elevated blood pressure, she insisted it was high and wanted to begin medication for hypertension right away.

This was all a little overwhelming and I became more confused by the variety of new concerns being presented. Other than the two seizures, Divot seemed healthy. In fact, both dogs were thoroughly examined and blood panels done just weeks before we moved and each had received a good report. Still nothing pointed to why she was having seizures.

An idiopathic seizure is described, as one in which there seems to be no detectable underlying cause. Considering some of this surprising information, and the opinions offered, I began to have some doubts. I wanted a second opinion and of course, we wanted to have Divot under the care of a neurologist so we asked for a referral. An appointment was made with Dr. Bob Bergman of Carolina Veterinary Specialists.

After reviewing Divot's health history, and the most recent report from the referring vet, and the notes I had taken, Dr. Bergman did not think that the seizures were due to heart or other organ issues. He explained that seizures in elderly dogs are unfortunately not all that rare, but there can be any number of underlying causes. During our conversation, I mentioned to him that over the past several months, Divot had seemed occasionally "spacey" often standing in one spot, staring at nothing. I thought perhaps it was old age and the beginning of some cognitive deficiencies. During Dr. Bergman's exam, he discovered that Divot was having two types of seizures – the obvious grand mal that we had witnessed, and also a type he called a "partial seizure."

The partial seizure is often barely noticeable, and in Divot's case, her partial seizures appeared to be only a quick, occasional wince. Having observed Divot having a partial seizure, Dr. Bergman asked me if I had seen this "wincing" before. I told him that it had started when we were still living in Arizona, but in the dry air, we (human and dog) were always getting static shocks, and I thought it might be attributed to the dry air. I told him that I did not recall seeing her do it as much lately. He asked if there was anything else unusual and I said, "Sometimes when she's settling down and getting comfortable, it sounds like she's grinding her teeth."

The options presented for our consideration were: 1) An MRI, but our concern was that Divot would need to be anesthetized and at nearly 13 years of age, it would be very hard on her already stressed system. 2) If we did the MRI and found a tumor, would we consider putting her through chemo, radiation, or surgery? 3) We could do the MRI and find nothing at all and still have no answers. We all decided that getting the seizures stopped immediately was of the utmost importance, and we discussed available medication options. All factors considered, we opted not to have an MRI right away, and started the anti-seizure medication immediately.

Divot's medication made her tired and lethargic but not too tired to beg. Here she is sliding under Nigel, though neither seems to notice.

Feeling like I had just had a lot of information dumped into my head, and quite fearful and overwhelmed, I started doing some additional research on seizures of both types, and I spoke with knowledgeable breeder friends who were well acquainted with Norwich Terrier health. Highly respected, Chicago based veterinary neurologist Dr. Michael Podell, DVM had recently given a seminar at the National Club's meeting. I found the following regarding partial seizures on his website, "*...partial seizures are the result of a focal abnormal electrical event in the brain. This seizure type may be associated with a higher prevalence of focal diseases* *such as a tumor. Animals with simple partial seizures have a sudden change in activity without any change in awareness, such as twitching of facial muscles. Animals with complex partial seizures often show unusual behavioral activity, such as running wildly around the house."*[1]

Considering the similarities between Dr. Bergman's findings and report, and Dr. Podell's article, I knew that Divot's condition was very serious.

Zonisamide was prescribed for the grand mal seizures. Dr. Bergman hoped that both types of seizure could be addressed with this one medication, but despite larger doses, the seizures continued. He then prescribed an additional medication, Keppra, to address the partial seizures. With the addition of the Keppra, the partial seizures subsided somewhat, but still the grand-mal seizures continued. I had begun to keep a seizure journal after Divot's second seizure and I continued to record and report to Dr. Bergman, and he adjusted her medication dosages as needed. I looked for patterns in her seizures, but just when it appeared that a pattern was developing, something would change. The only patterns that seemed to be developing with any consistency were: seizures happened mostly at night, after a seizure her left side usually showed weakness, and she would pace after nighttime seizures.

After a seizure, known as the post-ictal period, Divot was compelled to pace. During post-ictal pacing, it seemed that she would choose a particular path, and would seemingly run blindly back and forth upon the imaginary path. If something was in her way she did not go around it, she walked over it, stumbling, but not deterred. She would not be held and comforted in this post-ictal period, and if I did try to hold her, she struggled to free herself. She was compelled to pace and nothing could stop her. Divot's post-ictal pacing could last 20 minutes to two hours, until both her body and brain wound down. As they did, her pace too would begin to slow like little toy, its batteries finally drained. Only then could she stop and sleep. Watching her was both exhausting and heartbreaking.

In the quiet of the night, the rest of our neighborhood seemed so peaceful as I could only sit by helplessly and watch my sweet little friend first suffer the ravages of a seizure, and then watch her endless, exhausting pacing. The seizures were becoming more frequent, sometimes two weeks apart and sometimes less. The amount of medication Divot was on left her lethargic, but still did not stop the seizures as we'd hoped. She now seemed more like a stuffed animal than our once active, curious, and quirky Divot. My mind kept drifting back to Nigel's experience and the Phoenix neurologist's words echoed in my mind, *"If he doesn't get better, then we're going to know."*

During this time, I decided to take Divot to another vet for a second opinion about her blood pressure. I certainly didn't want to have her on any medications that were not completely necessary. I consulted with Dr. Bart Bryan of Independence Veterinary Clinic here in Charlotte. He agreed with Dr. Bergman that a heart problem would not cause seizures, especially two different *types* of seizures. Also, he was confused about some of the information contained in the previous vet's hand scrawled reports. Dr. Bryan wanted to do regular checks on Divot's blood pressure to see if she did indeed require medication. He found her blood pressure to be perfect – not high at all, but during these visits he allowed us to sit in a quiet room for a little while so that Divot could relax, and he could get a reading on her blood pressure under more normal circumstances. I appreciated his common sense approach, and his gentle way with Divot. When I introduced Nigel to him, he was very understanding about his vet fears and stayed completely calm, even having a few tricks up his sleeve to distract Nigel! Always feeling the need to apologize for Nigel's fear and the difficulties it caused for a simple exam, his response was, "I'll tell you what – I would be pretty scared if someone took me to a place where nobody spoke my language and they started poking and prodding me without my permission!" We had both Divot and Nigel's records transferred to Dr. Bryan's office immediately.

By mid November, Divot's seizures were becoming more frequent. The duration of several of her seizures was slightly longer than two minutes. In mid December, she had a seizure that lasted four minutes. At four minutes, we thought it was over but she let out a peculiar sound, like a quick scream, followed by another, and then another, and then she was quiet and the seizure was over. She remained rigid in my arms, for a few minutes more. By the time all body movements had stopped, the total time of the episode was nine minutes. The changes we were seeing were frightening. We continued to report to Dr. Bergman, and change her medication dosages as instructed. We tried to stay hopeful.

Both Mike and I became concerned about leaving Divot alone. I could not bear the thought of her having a seizure and me not being able to offer her help and comfort. Our other concern was Nigel. Though he had never shown any reaction to her seizures, I had been warned that when you have a dog who suffers seizures, there is always a chance that other dogs in the household could attack it. That is nature's way of keeping the weak away from the pack. While horrifying to us, it is nature and it should be respected. Never forget your dog is an animal first, and then your pet. We rarely left Divot alone at this point, but on the rare occasion that we both needed to be away, it was only for a very short time and we separated Nigel and Divot. In nearly 10 years together they had never been kept apart and now for both their sakes, they had to be.

The four of us had been through so much together, both good times and bad times. We had moved across country without knowing a soul (twice), having only each other, but it was always enough. We lived, worked, played, and traveled together. We had seen Nigel through life threatening illness and watched him bounce back, practically shaking his paw in defiance. But, here we were in yet another new place, alone again with a very, dark cloud hovering over our little family.

Nigel has her back. Nigel gives Divot the large dog bed but stays close.

~Teachable Moment~
Living with a dog who suffers seizures.

When you live with a dog who suffers seizures, the first thing you must remember to do is stay calm. Your dog's seizures may be hardly detectable, or may involve paddling, thrashing, drooling and the voiding of bladder and/or bowels. Your calmness will enable you to be an effective reporter to your vet and it will be much more beneficial to your dog than you being upset.

If your dog suffers a convulsive seizure:

- Stay calm.
- Make note of the time of the seizure onset, the length of the seizure and what happens to your dog during the seizure. Observe eyes, face, and body – all movements.
- It is an individual choice if you want to hold your dog or be near during a seizure. Be aware that it is possible that *any* dog could bite during a seizure episode.
- Be aware that some dogs may void bladder and/or bowels during, or immediately after a seizure.
- Be aware that there may be post-ictal activity. You probably cannot stop this activity but make sure your dog is safe. Block stairs, etc.
- For a first time seizure, you will want to get your dog to a vet immediately for a thorough exam. He or she will do a full physical and will most likely recommend a veterinary neurologist for further diagnostic testing and treatment.
- Keep a seizure journal and record your observations while information is still fresh in your mind. Share it with your dog's neurologist as soon as possible.
- Once your dog has suffered a seizure, if you have more than one dog, it would be advisable to separate them when you are not at home.
- If a seizure lasts longer than 5-10 minutes, seek veterinary care immediately. Long seizures (longer than 20-30 minutes) can be life threatening. Also, if your pet experiences cluster seizures (more than one seizure in a 24 hour period), or does

not regain consciousness, seek veterinary treatment immediately.[2]

~Teachable Moment~
There is always another opinion.

I have talked to and met with many vets in the past 13 years due to the relocations we have made. Some I have really liked and respected and some I did not. Don't get me wrong; I think a veterinarian's job is incredibly difficult. He or she has a patient who cannot tell them anything about the problem they are having, and it is often a matter of a little poking and manipulating to begin diagnosis, and moving on to diagnostic equipment if the physical exam proves inconclusive. Some vets have a great way with dogs and a not-so-great way with the human, or visa versa. When making your decision to choose a veterinarian, you the human also have to make a connection with the vet. You are your dog's advocate, and you are the one who lives with your dog and knows him better than anyone else. If you do not feel heard or feel respected by your veterinarian, you should seek out another vet. If you do not feel confident that a particular vet has the latest information and training, you should seek out another vet. Your dog depends on you to make every decision for him and this is one of the most important ones. It is never too late to switch vets or at *least* seek a second opinion!

A NORWICH TALE

Tales of Old – November 2010

Bittersweet are the golden years.

When your puppy is young and silly you think he'll never mature, especially when you are working on milestones such as housebreaking and teaching him the proper use of his sharp little teeth (yes Nigel I'm talking about you). When Nigel and Divot were robust young adults, they were so full of themselves – so energetic, and always ready to go! I could never imagine them being any other way. I could never imagine them not being able to keep up with *me.*

Playtime has gone from constant, to infrequent, to nonexistent. What used to look like two furry slot cars racing around the house has been replaced by what looks more like two tiny, furry rugs at my feet. Nigel has become the amble-around-the-yard type rather than the hiking-in-the-mountains type he was not so long ago. In addition to her natural slow down, Divot's anti-seizure medication makes her a little dull and lethargic. But just a few days ago, everything was just right; she must have been feeling really good, because she had a little burst of energy accompanied by one of her old pop and spin moves, and a quick sprint. It did not last long but it sure made us smile to see her like that again.

Some of their senses are beginning to dull just as senses do in every aging creature, although if there is any activity coming from the kitchen, sharpness and clarity miraculously return. The good manners they once possessed such as sitting quietly for their food, or staying out from underfoot in the kitchen have all but disappeared. They can no longer understand my instruction but that is okay. They did as I asked when they could, but now the only thing that is important is keeping them safe. I must be extra careful in the kitchen from now on.

Everything that involves Nigel and Divot takes much longer these days. A trip outside can take a remarkably long time to get both dogs down the "geriatric doggie ramp," through the garage, and out the door to the lawn to do their business. Sometimes Nigel goes to the wrong side of the door and he cannot for the life of him figure out why I am trying to get him to go out the other side of the door – the *open* side. Sometimes I just pick him up and place him in front of the open door. *There you go buddy, straight out from here now.* This is the beginning of dementia. In the meantime Divot dawdles, making her way to the door, sniffing carefully along the carpeted runway in the garage. Despite my encouragement, she is in no hurry.

Divot is still as lovely as she was in her youth,
and Nigel is still as handsome as ever, in The Golden Years.

Finally outside, they do their business and now we repeat the whole process to come back in. Once up the ramp they stop and stand in the open doorway to the house. Perhaps they do this because I am standing in the open doorway, but since I am the only one of the three of us who can open or shut a door, I have good reason to be standing there. After much encouragement and a little prodding from me, they finish walking through the door and come into the house. I am living with a hairy little geriatric couple that does not speak English…

Nigel has the uncanny ability to know when it is four o'clock wherever he is, and he demands to eat right then. During our travels, we have gone through three different time zones in a matter of a few days and when the clock hits 4:00 p.m., no matter where we are, it is time to eat according to Nigel. This is the doggie version of The Early Bird Special. *Its 4:00 and it's time for my dinner!* Like some older folks I know (yes Dad, I'm talking about you), they eat because it is time, not because they are necessarily hungry. Nigel either knows how to read a clock, or his internal clock switches over at cell towers like my phone does. I also believe he came equipped with GPS but that's another tale.

This can all be a little frustrating at times but it is incredibly sweet, and incredibly sad. It seems that our time together has been relatively short and yet they have changed so much. I have reminisced lately about the wonderful trips we have taken with Nigel and Divot. We have seen beautiful scenery, and hiked some amazing trails together. I wouldn't trade those high-energy times for anything, and yet I wouldn't trade these slower, gentle times either. I have always thought of Nigel and Divot as being like my children – not that I think they are human – I respect them as the wonderful canines they are – but my children in a sense that I am responsible for keeping them safe, meeting their needs, teaching them, and taking care of them each and every day of their lives. But suddenly I am forced to see them as very elderly beings. One day, my "children" became so old, and it has required quite a mental leap to adjust. I can only hope that I am wise enough to meet their changing needs and do what is right to help them through the next phase. For now, we are treasuring each day and taking it slow.

Chapter 13
Lost Love

THE UNHAPPIEST NEW YEAR OF ALL

Nigel knew before we knew. On the day that turned out to be Divot's last day, we knew that she was very ill, but Nigel knew that his best friend was dying.

New Year's Day 2011 started early for us as most days had for a while. Divot's sleep patterns were really not patterns at all anymore. She was driven to get up anywhere between 4:00-4:30 a.m., and sometimes earlier, so we were up and starting a new day and a new year. After the usual outing we settled in for morning coffee. The weather had turned a little warmer after a few cold and wet days. Though it was still a cloudy day, and having a little cabin fever, we decided to put Nigel and Divot in the car and go for a drive in the country. We thought maybe we could even find a place to let them out to explore if Divot was up to it, but she slept the entire time we were out. She usually enjoyed looking out the window for at least a little while but she slept soundly during the entire outing.

After a short, uneventful trip, by midday, Mike and I were tired from lack of sleep and we decided to hunker down for a nap. Divot slept soundly next to me and when I awoke a little while later, she barely stirred as I picked her up and carried her to the living room. There I cuddled with her, and let the cobwebs clear from my still tired mind. She continued to sleep but not in her usual way, which was to stretch out lengthwise on my lap. Instead, she curled *into* me. It was as if she was trying to get as close and small as possible. She stayed this way for a few more hours. I did not have the heart to move her so I stayed put holding her and petting her, allowing her to sleep. Finally at four o'clock with Nigel's internal dinner bell ringing, her eyes slowly opened and she sat up. I could tell right away that something was wrong. She was weak and seemed somewhat disoriented. I put her on the floor to get a better idea of what might be going on, but she was very unsteady so I held her while I got their food ready. I was unsure if she would eat when I placed her at her bowl. She did eat, but not with her usual gusto and she swayed noticeably as she ate. Wondering if maybe her blood sugar had suddenly plunged, I gave her a teaspoon of vanilla ice cream. Some 30 minutes later she had perked up a little but she was still not acting at all close to normal.

At 5:30 p.m. as we were in the kitchen preparing our own dinner, Divot suddenly fell onto her side and began to have a seizure. The pattern that had emerged was that they mostly occurred when she was sleeping, so this was rather unusual. In comparison to previous seizures however, it was a fairly mild one, and it did not last long – less than a minute. Afterward, her recovery was more rapid than in previous instances, and she seemed to have no after effects, not even the pacing. We thought that maybe the new medication protocol was working or at least trending that way. We actually felt hope for the first time in a long time. The rest of the evening was uneventful as both dogs slept peacefully in their chosen places. But just after midnight, our feelings of hope were suddenly dashed. Divot began having another seizure. This one lasted for about three minutes, which was unusually long compared to most of the previous ones. This change in activity immediately raised our concerns. Just when we thought the episode was ending, she began to thrash about and pant very hard and very loudly, her tongue turning bright red. It was as if another wave of seizure with completely different symptoms was washing over her. We had never seen *this* before. Fearing hyperthermia, I stepped outside into the cool, dark night and held her, speaking gently and calmly, but she could not stop panting. I brought her back inside and held a cool cloth to her tummy, her face, and armpits hoping to aid the cooling process. Then she began to vocalize…

"Vocalize" is a term used in the discussion of seizures when the victim makes involuntary sounds. It has been explained to me that the sounds, being involuntary, do not mean the animal is in pain, but the sounds that were coming from sweet Divot were like the sickening sounds of an animal being slaughtered. It was hard to imagine that she was not in excruciating pain *somewhere.* The thrashing and non-stop screaming continued, and because Divot had not experienced a seizure of this magnitude, we headed to the emergency vet. I called to let them know we were on our way, almost screaming into the phone to compete with Divot's screaming. By the time we arrived some 20 minutes later, she had calmed down a little. They took her in immediately for an examination.

As Mike paced around the waiting room, I noticed that another woman was there, and she was alone. We were the only ones in the waiting room. I felt numb. I knew I should say something to her – it was the right thing to do. I tried to gather my thoughts and get my emotions under control before going to her. When you find yourself at an emergency vet hospital in the middle of the night and there are other people there, you know that you all have something awful in common. Before I could get up and go to her, suddenly she approached me and sat down next to me handing me a tissue. She put her arm around me and said, "I'm sorry for whatever you're going through honey. I'm sure they'll be able to help your little dog." I hugged her back and thanked her and wished her well with her dog too. We sat there together for a few moments saying nothing else. We did not talk about the reasons we were there, nor did we introduce ourselves. It wasn't necessary. We were two strangers united in crisis. Until now, I had not thought of her since that night but whoever she was, she renewed my hope in humanity and I could never thank her enough for her selfless act, and her generosity amidst her own despair. *The kindness of strangers…*

I have no idea how long we waited, but eventually a tech came out and escorted us to a room and shortly after, the veterinarian on staff came in to update us on Divot's condition. He told us that Divot had been given some Valium and that she had stopped seizing but her neurological functions were diminished. He explained to us that that while her eyes were reacting to light stimulus, he could not say with any confidence that her brain was able to interpret the stimulus – that she was actually "seeing." He added that sometimes these functions do return, but only time would tell. He asked if we would like to leave her there for the weekend, but not wanting to cause her anymore undo stress, I told him that we would take her home and have her see Dr. Bergman on Monday. He said he would forward his report to him right away so it would be there Monday. I could not imagine her having another major seizure in such a short time span, but I asked if there was anything we could give her along with her regular medication protocol to get through the weekend just in case. He offered a syringe of Valium to administer rectally if another major seizure should occur, but warned that the medication in the syringe would be viable for only 12 hours. We all hoped we wouldn't need it. When the tech returned Divot to us, he gently placed her on the table, where she seemed to melt onto it, unable to even stand. She was a little black and tan puddle. Even the young tech looked moved by her plight, and he quietly mouthed, "I'm sorry." I sobbed as I picked up my precious friend and we brought her home.

THE BREAK OF DAWN

I sent Mike and Nigel to bed and stayed up with Divot. She was now agitated as was often the case after a nighttime seizure and she paced on and off. Tonight however due to her diminished sight, she was running into furniture and even falling down. I feared she might hurt herself, so I tried to hold her. She would allow it only for a few moments and then she wanted to be released.

Always ravenous after a seizure, I thought that perhaps some food might help to settle her down. As I offered her some bits of scrambled egg from my hand, she frantically seemed to be looking for the food though my hand was right under her nose. Finally, she found the food and gobbled it up. Her ability to see had not returned. She paced some more and dozed a little here and there but did not sleep soundly, as I had hoped she would. At 5:00 a.m., her core instincts kicking in, on wobbly legs, she tried to eat breakfast with Nigel. Again, it was more like going through the motions but she did eat. She had to be held up with the aid of her harness to relieve herself. She was weak and still seemed very disoriented. Wanting someone to stay awake to monitor Divot, and knowing I was not going to sleep, I sent Mike and Nigel back to bed. Divot slept on my lap, finally resting. As I held Divot and watched her breathe, I gently rubbed her little ears, and wondered what the day might bring. Though my mind was exhausted and foggy, hundreds of memories flooded my brain. I never took one moment for granted with her. I loved her more than words could possibly say.

Several hours later Mike and Nigel emerged from the bedroom, and I took my turn to sleep. Though I tried to slow down my thoughts, sleep would not come. The signs were ominous. Something was happening to Divot and it was happening very quickly. What should I do? What *could* I do? No answers came, only the sickening fear that I was losing her. Was she in pain? That was not something either of us could bear. What if she never regained her sight? At nearly 13 years of age, could she handle, suddenly being thrust into a dark world? Her quality of life on large doses of anti-seizure drugs was already questionable. She had become a mere shell of the dog she had once been. The feelings of helplessness, sadness, anger, and frustration surfaced. I wanted to scream. Instead I sobbed. Somehow I knew that every precious moment with Divot mattered. After 15 minutes I got up.

When I came into the living room Divot was sleeping next to Mike on the sofa. I sat down and gently picked her up and laid her on my chest. She continued to sleep. I asked, "How is she doing? Has she been sleeping?" He answered, "She's been kind of agitated on and off. At first she wanted to get down and walk around but she's still really unstable. I'm afraid she's going to hurt herself." He continued, "After you went to bed, she wanted to get down from my lap. She was pretty insistent. I thought maybe she wanted to look for you so I put her down, but she kept trying to go to Nigel. But every time she got close to him, he walked away from her. I still don't think she can see well, if at all, but for some reason he does *not* want to be near her." After being rebuffed by Nigel several times Divot rested and Nigel crawled back under his favorite end table and slept.

At around 10:00.am. Nigel awoke, stretched, and looked around and then asked to go outside. Mike took him out, but after doing his business he did not want to come back in. Finally Mike had to pick him up and carry him in. He said that Nigel looked nervous and frightened when told to come in, holding his head down and his ears flat. Finally back in the house, Nigel tentatively came into the living room where Divot and I were, and then, with ears flat, and tail tucked, he anxiously left the room, retreating to Mike's office at the far end of the house. He was restless and anxious, and could not seem to settle down, and we became increasingly concerned about him. He asked to go out several more times, and once outside, he refused to come back in on his own. He returned to the living room one more time and anxiously looked at Divot and then he crept away, wanting to go outside or anywhere – just away from *her*.

As I thought about his odd behavior, my first thought was *"Is he getting sick?"* But Nigel was showing signs of *fear* not illness. It was then that a horrible thought occurred to me. I said to Mike, "Nigel is frightened and his flight mechanism is definitely on. There's something about Divot that he's afraid of."

As we were contemplating this frightening new thought, Divot suddenly sat up and a rapid series of partial seizures hit her – five or six in a row – something that had never happened before. I knew in that instant she was going to have another seizure, and as feared, her little body was again racked with convulsions and then panting. While Mike held her I administered the Valium and hoped it would be effective. It wasn't. She began to drool thick mucous and as she breathed, she suddenly sounded wet. She was making a gurgling sound, and I was afraid she was choking. I tipped her body up with her head down, patting and firmly rubbing her back, and some of the mucous came out, which made her sound much clearer. The convulsions continued and then the hideous sounding vocalizations began. I clenched my teeth and shut my eyes as tightly as I could, as if it would somehow stop the sickening sound. Mike and I looked at each other through our tears, each of us feeling defeated. How could we ask Divot to endure one more minute like this? How many more seizures would she endure until a new medication protocol could be found? It could take weeks or maybe months. Was it even possible to help her? How much could her brain and little body endure? Once again, the words of Nigel's vet echoed in my mind, *"If he doesn't get better, then we're going to know."*

We had always agreed that we would do everything possible to provide our dogs with a loving and safe home. We believe that there are things that are the normal course of care for an aging dog, but then there are things that we believe force them to stay in bodies that no longer want to be present. We had always agreed that no matter how difficult it would be to say good-bye, we would do all that we could, and then allow Nigel and Divot to go with the dignity they deserved. We had that discussion again the previous night on the way home from the E-vet. Now we were being called to act on our convictions. After the things Divot had experienced, neither of us felt that her quality of life was good, and we both knew that she was suffering. Once in the car, I called the E-vet again and told them we were on our way. The drive there was excruciating. The pitiful, thrashing, screaming animal I held in my arms seemed so far removed from my happy, sweet, and loving Divot. Though I spoke softly, calmly and reassuringly to her, inside I was screaming. *"SHE DOES NOT DESERVE THIS! SHE DOES NOT DESERVE THIS!"*

She was still in full-blown seizure when we arrived 20 minutes later. Though the waiting room was full, a tech met us at the door, took Divot from my arms, and immediately rushed her to the back, away from the other dogs. The vet came out and after discussing the events of the previous night with her, we told her of our decision to let Divot go. She did not hesitate and said, "I understand. She's being given something to calm down right now. Please come with me." She ushered us to a comfortable, room and said, "I'll bring her in to you in a few minutes." With kindness and compassion, she brought Divot back to us in a blanket and gently laid her on my lap, whispering, "Take all the time you need with her."

Divot lay on my lap, sedated and finally peaceful – much different from the writhing, pitiful creature we walked in with. There, we said all that we wanted to say to her. We spoke of the fun times: watching her chase chipmunks, wrestling and roughhousing with Nigel, traveling together, hiking in beautiful places, and the joy of living every day with the sweetest, most loving, quirky being that ever was. We spoke of so many other treasured moments we had committed to memory. Every day we had spent with Divot was a joy. It was that simple.

As she lay on my lap, I stroked her head and massaged her once muscular, once sturdy little body, so frail feeling now. Her face, still beautiful to me, suddenly looked like that belonging to an ancient being. We thanked her for the joy she had given us, and told her over and over how much we loved her, hoping she could still sense it.

I didn't want to call the doctor back in. I wanted to stay there, holding her and looking at her, memorizing every detail, and yet I knew that with each passing moment I held on to her, I was becoming weaker. My resolve to end her suffering was weakening, as my selfish desire to keep her was taking over. I wanted to get this over with, and yet I knew that the moment it was over, never again would I hear her raspy bark or hear her funny squirrel-like chatter. I would never again have the joy of holding this sweet, wonderful creature, or feel her warm, gentle lick upon my cheek. I kissed her soft little ears one more time and whispered my own personal thoughts to her. When the strength came, we summoned the doctor.

Moments later as I held Divot, she fell asleep peacefully on my lap, and she breathed her last breath, finally free from a body that had begun to betray her in a most horrible way.

Me and my girl. San Diego Dog Beach, December 2006.

THE PERFECT NATURE OF NATURE

One thing you cannot do is fool a dog. You can act brave when you're frightened, or you can act happy when you're sad, but really you cannot "act" anything that you don't feel in front of a dog. I had learned *that* many years ago.

When we arrived home from the E-vet a few hours later, as anyone would, we made a feeble attempt to do just that; we tried to try to fool Nigel into thinking that everything was fine. We came in saying what we always do upon returning home, and Mike took him out to potty as one of us always does. When they came back in I squatted down to pet Nigel and scratch his chin, saying what I always do, "Hey buddy, did you have a good nap?" But Nigel showed the same fear I had seen in him that morning. His ears and tail went down and he moved away from me. Though his behavior was upsetting, I thought I understood. Maybe he was sensing my emotional turmoil, and he needed to withdraw from me. I could understand that. I may have been partly right but I was partly wrong.

As the afternoon went on, we numbly tried to process all that had happened. Nigel continued to avoid me, but then something about his peculiar behavior came into focus in my mind. I was still wearing the clothes that I wore that morning. While Nigel may have not wanted to be near me in my highly charged emotional state, perhaps he was reacting to something else, something more physical. I put my clothes into the washer and drew a hot bath. And just as he had done for every bath I have ever taken since he was a young dog, Nigel came in and lay next to the bathtub, curling up on the rug. For Nigel, for now, the world was right again.

Nigel reminded me about the perfect nature of nature that day. Of the two coping mechanisms a dog has – fight or flight – Nigel's natural response to fear or other discomforts has always been flight. True to his nature, Nigel was trying to flee what only he could sense was happening – the coming of Divot's devastating seizure – and I believe that he sensed that his pack mate was dying. After that, he tried to flee the scent of death I carried upon my clothes. Looking back, if there was anything good to be taken from that day, it was that I was reminded of the perfect nature of nature, and given a glimpse into the very powerful, instinctual, sensory world of a dog.

GOOD GRIEF

I am not sure what was more difficult – trying to cope with our own grief over losing Divot, or watching Nigel grieve for her. I had never witnessed an animal grieving. In many ways, it was really not so different from ours.

The day that Divot passed was so emotionally overwhelming and chaotic, when we finally did settle in that evening, Nigel, who had barely slept all day, fell asleep immediately when we settled down. It wasn't until the next day that we began to see signs of his grief. He walked around the house slowly, stopping frequently to listen. He didn't nap at his usual times and in his usual places, but continued to look and listen for Divot. During the workday, Nigel and Divot both usually stayed in my office sleeping in their favorite spots, but in the days just after Divot's passing, Nigel went restlessly back and forth between Mike's office and mine. For days he continued to look and listen for her, going from room to room. Sometimes he would lie under his favorite table or on his bed in our bedroom, not sleeping, just staring into space as if trying to understand the sudden emptiness.

Divot was the only dog he was ever completely comfortable with, and the only other being in our household who completely understood him. If there exists such a thing as the ability of dogs to feel love for each other, I believe Nigel and Divot did love each other. But now she was gone, ripped from him as suddenly as she was ripped from us. If a broken heart can break even more, mine did, watching Nigel grieve for his one and only friend.

In the days following, Nigel's appetite remained normal but he was more sedate, as if he was just going through the motions. We gave him affection when he wanted it, did what we could to distract him, and when we needed to let our emotions out, we went away from him. After about two weeks he stopped looking and listening for Divot and his mood even lightened a bit. After that he still had moments where he would go off alone in the bedroom and checking in on him, I would find him lying awake on his bed as if pondering something. I would sit near him and stroke his head trying to offer comfort as best I could, and then I would leave him alone to work through it. Nigel grieved his friend honestly and completely, without shame, without concerns of time, and without "what ifs." He grieved Divot as his nature intended, and then he moved on.

As for you the human, your own grief is an important part of this process. Shedding tears is nothing to be ashamed of and when you feel moved to cry over the loss of your friend, you should allow yourself to do so without shame. The emotions you feel, such as disbelief, guilt, sadness, and anger, are normal. Talk to trusted friends and family members. Most people have had a dog and have been where you are or will be where you are, and they will understand and some will share your grief. Do not set time limits on yourself for what is "right" or "wrong" in the grieving process, as there is no such thing. I have spoken with people who still shed tears many years after their dog has passed. You have loved and lost – it is real and it is painful.

There are many helpful organizations that have experienced grief counselors who can also help you during this difficult time. Your vet can recommend someone in your area. Give yourself permission to grieve in the way you need to. Be kind to yourself.

~Teachable Moment~
The Grieving Dog

I believe that dogs grieve. When two or more dogs live together and one dies, the remaining dog will most likely show signs of grief. This can be displayed as a loss of appetite, barking more or barking less, looking for the deceased companion, development of separation anxiety, or other unwanted behavior changes. Grief is normal and natural, but if loss of appetite or unusual eliminations should develop, you should discuss this with your veterinarian. If prolonged, inappropriate behaviors continue, along with seeing your vet, you may consider enlisting a behaviorist to guide you and your dog through the grieving process. Sometimes your own emotional state can contribute to behavioral problems, so be sure you are finding proper outlets for your grief and not contributing to the problem.

If your dog thrives on routine, you can help him or her by keeping to the normal routine. If he or she has an activity that they love, such as going for a walk, be sure to do that several times a day to change the focus. Since Nigel thrives on a routine, we knew we had to try to keep his routine for his well-being. We added several short walks each day to distract him, and to get him out into the fresh air. Being out and seeing friendly neighbors certainly helped him too. If unusual behaviors develop, such as barking or whining, do not reinforce them by giving attention or treats at that time, as you will only be reinforcing a new and unwanted behavior.

If you have a dog who thrives on change and adventure, then you will want to include him or her in more of your activities. One Norwich Terrier breeder told me that when her elderly Norwich female died, the son of the dog was devastated. "We watched him withdraw from the family and we were very concerned about him. He would lie in his dog bed and look at the wall. Nothing worked until we started to do some new things with him that we had not done before. He went to work with my husband, and we started some new 'chores' for him like garbage can duty, mailbox runs, and trips to the hardware store. This seemed to finally lift his spirits."

Each dog is an individual. Just like us humans, each being grieves in its own way. It seems that the steady application of time is the only balm that soothes and heals the wounds of loss.

A NORWICH TALE

Completely Wonderful Divot – March 2011

She completed us.

You have probably heard the now famous line "You complete me" from the 1996 movie Jerry McGuire. This sentiment may not only have been true for the fictional Jerry McGuire, but it was also true for Nigel. Actually, it was true for all of us.

Before Divot came, Nigel had been an "only dog" for three years. He had come to us as a 13-1/2 week old puppy, and since we did not have many friends who had dogs back then, Nigel lacked interaction with other dogs, causing him to be a little socially inept to say the least. For three years, while being in a loving home, with doting people, he was in a sense, very much alone. There was no other being in the house who he could completely relate to, completely understand, or who completely understood *him.* Then along came Divot – someone who was like him! When Nigel met Divot, there was an immediate connection. He *really* liked her, he trusted her, and he was very attracted to her. Divot, having spent her first three years with other dogs at the breeder's house, knew how to be social and had a first hand experience in a pack environment. This was the kind of experience that Nigel lacked, and Divot helped him to experience all of these things. In her presence Nigel blossomed. They were constant companions from the very first day. I believe Divot helped him to fulfill his "dog-ness." Divot completed him.

My favorite photo of Divot, taken when she was five years old.

For Mike and me, the addition of Divot to our family brought us sweetness that we had never known before. Nigel, always an independent boy, accepted cuddling and affection on his own terms; he was not comfortable lying on a lap or being held too close, but Divot… Divot could not get enough affection. She relished in being held close, cuddled and petted. She was the perfect Norwich Terrier – running off to chase a squirrel or other varmint one minute, snuggling in close, soaking up all the affection she could get the next minute. She fulfilled that need for us.

When Divot passed, our home and hearts were left with a void, both physical and emotional. This little one who had given so much to each one of us, and who had forever changed us all, was suddenly gone. In the end, perhaps she did what she was meant to do. She completed us.

Chapter 14
Seasons of Change

THE HEALING GARDEN

In the almost 10 years that Divot was with us, I had hardly ever been away from her but for a few days in any given year. I think of her daily and I still miss her terribly. It feels like a piece of my own being has been ripped from me. She passed in the gloom of winter, on the second day of the New Year, 2011 and though it is spring now, I still miss her as much as I did the day we let her go. It seems like forever since I have seen her sweet face, felt her warmth, and heard her squirrel-like chatter. There are still not many days that I am not reduced to tears for at least a few moments as the sadness overwhelms me. Because of the sudden loss of Divot, sometimes when I look at pictures of her I find myself asking, *"Was any of this real?"*

Spring in North Carolina is in one word, *breathtaking*. Each day is a beautiful miracle. For us, the arid desert climate of Arizona was quite a change from the lush green springs and summers of Michigan, and during our six years in Arizona, the gardening options left landscape enthusiasts like us, a little less than satisfied. Now back in a climate much more suitable to our love for landscape projects, we spend a great deal of time nurturing our yard and gardens.

Shortly after Divot's passing we decided to plant a memorial garden in her honor. Flowers have always reminded me of Divot. When we lived in Michigan we had flowerbeds or potted arrangements everywhere, and they often served as a backdrop for many of our photos of Nigel and Divot. The idea of creating something that would be a living and ever-changing place of beauty just seemed like the right thing to do to celebrate the life of, and honor the memory of our special little friend.

The little garden was completed a few weeks ago, and while not exactly a joyous experience to create, in having completed this labor of love, we began to feel a sense of peace. The garden contains a fountain, Mandevilla vines with large red, white, and pink flowers, and is also populated with small, bright, cheery flowers, many of which we had in our Michigan landscape. Also, a small sign reads, "WELCOME DIVOT'S GARDEN."

I guess in many ways, trying to recapture the familiar is my way of paying homage to, or reclaiming the past. A time when both dogs were young and vibrant, when Divot, my loyal and constant companion was with me, and the four of us were together, surrounded by many loved ones. It was the best time of my life.

The little garden is in a way, a microcosm of the realities of life. There is life, growth, then death. There is movement and stillness. There is plenty and drought. There is beauty and ugliness. There are things that are beyond our control no matter what we do to stop them. That is the nature of life. Despite the pain of losing Divot, I am grateful I was given the opportunity to experience the wonder of bonding so closely with an animal. Divot's garden is a living tribute to a special friend, and a truly great dog, and our small way of saying, "Thank you."

A NORWICH TALE
Wagging His Way Back – April 2011

Moving forward.

In the weeks following the devastating loss of Divot I knew that I had to help Nigel move on. While I wanted to keep his routine, I wanted to add something special to it. In an aging dog, your choices are somewhat limited so this means only one thing – a trip to Petsmart. Nigel and Divot had logged thousands of miles with us, and while there was always some out of control excitement by Nigel, there was never fear of being in the car. Lately when I put him in the car, he begins to shake and act fearful – something he has never done before. Maybe the last big trip was just too much for the old boy. But, if I wanted to spice up his life a little, I was going to have to help him work through it. So, I put him in the car and off we went to Petsmart. The poor little guy was shaking badly, but upon pulling into the parking lot, he got really excited. As is my practice now, I waited patiently and did not get out until he calmed down. Once out of the car, he headed straight for the door. He knew where he was! He saw all the people and his body language spoke of pure Norwich joy – he was wagging all over!

Nigel's technique to garner the most attention possible is to enter a store and take a look around to see if anyone has noticed that he has arrived. Sometimes he can get some attention from someone who is leaving the store, which is a fantastic way to begin his visit, really setting the tone. Then he begins to walk the aisles, choosing aisles where someone is present; aisles without people are of no interest to him. Nobody is a stranger to Nigel and it is his practice to walk up to every person he sees, look up at them with his entire body wagging, and see if they would like to pet him. Though people are shopping, reading labels, or speaking with store personnel, none of that seems to matter to him. I believe he is convinced that the real reason they are at the store is to see *him.* Most people see a small, cute, friendly dog and will stop to pet him, which pleases him greatly. He gets a pet, a scratch and an "Oh, such a cute little fellow," and then he moves on, as there are more aisles to explore and people who have not yet had their chance to meet him. On rare occasions, someone will ignore Nigel, which seems to both surprise and confuse him. He approaches everyone in the same way, so why doesn't his charm work on everyone? Could they be…*cat people*? When he finally understands that someone will not be forthcoming with attention, he moves on, always glancing back and I know he is thinking, *"What just happened here?"* This confusion lasts for only a moment or two until he spots the next person.

We walked all the aisles of Petsmart five or six times that day, until he had his fill. After his outing he was much more calm on the way home. Once home, he immediately went to his blanket and fell asleep, a very satisfied and tired dog.

Nigel, on his own again.

It was a bittersweet day for me. It was the first time that Nigel and I had been on an outing without Divot in nearly 10 years. Though painful, how could I not feel good about seeing Nigel so happy and clearly enjoying himself? By nature he lives without regrets and the memory of any crushing sadness. His frame of reference is the present. For Nigel there is no yesterday, and there is no concern for tomorrow. There is only now.

Chapter 15
Caring For the Elderly

CHANGE IS THE ONE CONSTANT THING

I suppose I should not be surprised by the changes I have seen in Nigel in recent months. After all, change is the one thing you can count on. It is just the *way* he has changed that is so surprising. Never having been a dog who craved affection, or as you may recall from an earlier chapter, never liking to be too close to anyone, especially face to face, he seems much more comfortable with it these days. While not constantly seeking affection, he has begun to do so, especially first thing in the morning and in the evening before he retires to bed. He still has his favorites, head and ear scratches and of course, rump rubs. Sometimes when I pick him up, he slowly and carefully sniffs my face, something he would never have been comfortable with in his youth. Certainly "kisses" were out of the question, but these days when I come home after being gone for several hours, he gets very excited and gives me kisses.

There is probably a logical explanation for all of this. Perhaps he feels more vulnerable and not so independent these days, or perhaps his dimming eyesight causes him to need to have a closer look than before, and the kisses... I have no explanation for what is behind that display of submission or affection. Perhaps it is the dementia that has altered his personality so. He *is* a different dog, but deep down, he is still Nigel.

As Nigel and Divot moved toward their golden years, I began to look for information about this new stage they were entering. There are many books available about caring for puppies but I have not seen much written on the subject of caring for the elderly dog. As Nigel and Divot entered this new stage, I was unsure about what to expect, and how to prepare myself to meet their changing needs and give them the best care possible. Considering that puppyhood is a relatively short time in your dog's life, and the geriatric period can last for several years, it is unfortunate that there is not more information available. To that end, this chapter, like all the others in this book, will be based solely on my own experiences with Nigel and Divot. I have also sought the guidance of our trusted veterinarian, Dr. Bart Bryan of Independence Veterinary Clinic here in Charlotte, NC.

From the various charts I have found, for a small dog like a Norwich Terrier, aging is approximately 5-1/2 years to our human year according to current estimates, though many charts adjust that number slightly at various stages of the dog's life. The old standard was 7:1 but that number is now usually applied to large breeds.

In the absence of major illness, the aging process reveals itself slowly. One day you notice that your friend is graying a little around the ears and muzzle. Then you begin to notice that he lacks the stamina he used to have for playtime and long walks. He begins to sleep more and play less. Eventually some of his senses may begin to dull. These are the senior years, and it is a special but a bittersweet time. Your adult Norwich used to be so active and confident! Now, he needs your help, patience, and understanding as much as he did when he was a puppy.

In our conversations about the aging process, Dr. Bryan has offered some thought-provoking ideas on the topic. Dr. Bryan reminds us that, "Age is not a disease. That would be unfair, as all older dogs are not 'sick.' Just as with humans, there is a better chance of illness and disease as dogs age, but age does not necessarily condemn a dog to illness."

As your Norwich begins to age, you may begin to notice:

- Sleeps more, plays less, or stops playing altogether.
- Moves slower or shows difficulty getting up, or appears stiff.
- Eyesight not as keen, sometimes eyes become cloudy.
- Some loss of hearing and possible loss of sense of smell.
- Tooth/breath problems develop.
- Digestive issues may develop.

- Has trouble with incontinence.
- Weight gain or loss.
- May show impatience or discomfort with grooming.
- Changes on the skin.
- Difficulty understanding and/or seems confused.

Let's look at some of these concerns more in depth:

Sleep

As your Norwich ages, he needs more sleep. Naps will become longer and more frequent. For Nigel and Divot, the increase in the need for sleep became noticeable around the age of nine, but they were still quick to awaken from a nap, sharp and ready for action. By the age of 12 though, both were sleeping most of the day and sleep was much deeper; both were notice-ably slower when waking up. When waking them, I would gently call their names to avoid startling them.

Exercise and Movement

It is important for all dogs to have some form of daily exercise. This not only helps keep weight in check, but movement is good for the muscles that support your dog's aging frame. In the case of an elderly dog, avoid long walks and try shorter more frequent outings instead. If your dog stops wanting to go for walks, do not force him, as he may be in pain, or he may have some fear, perhaps due to vision loss, or loss of some mental faculties. Nigel has recently begun refusing walks and instead prefers his slow "walkabouts" in his own yard. Be sure to speak with your veterinarian about how much exercise is appropriate for your individual dog, based on his current health. In a recent conversation, Dr. Bryan told me that in his experience, obesity is the most common "disease" he sees in older dogs. He cautions owners about the variety of complications that obesity causes, predisposing dogs to among other things, diabetes and arthritis. He says, "Arthritis makes it difficult for dogs to posture to urinate, defecate, and groom themselves." He adds, "Sadly, more dogs are euthanized due to arthritis than any other disease."

You may find that your elderly dog no longer enjoys or feels comfortable being picked up. Whether this is physical or mental discomfort, if he shows signs of discomfort, leave his feet on the floor and join him there so you can still enjoy closeness. If your dog has been your bed companion, as difficult as it may be, you may want to consider having him sleep on his own bed on the floor next to yours. Then you will not have to worry about him jumping off the bed and hurting himself. Don't worry, he will adapt to this change much easier than you will.

Hearing/Eyesight

At one time or another, we have all accused our Norwich of having "selective hearing," meaning they ignore us when something else is more interesting. As your dog ages, however, inability to hear can become real. You may think your elderly dog is ignoring you, but it is very possible he is suffering from hearing loss. In the case of Nigel and Divot at around the age of 12, they both began showing difficulty in discerning the *direction* sounds were coming from. This problem escalated when we moved to a new home. The change in environment could have been a contributing factor to their confusion. From my observations, I believe that the problem of discerning direction could be the result of actual hearing loss, sound bouncing off hard surfaces, or perhaps even an imbalance in the hearing ability in each ear. I have always tried to use hand signals along with verbal direction with Nigel and Divot for the eventuality of compromised hearing, and it has been helpful.

Loss of at least some hearing in an elderly dog is normal, just as it is in humans.

You may notice changes in your dog's eyes and eyesight as he ages. Eyes can begin to develop more tear matter, so be sure to gently wipe crusty eyes with a warm damp cloth. Eyes can become cloudy, which might indicate the presence of cataracts. Another common eye problem is nuclear sclerosis, (or lenticular sclerosis), as is the case with Nigel according to his vet in Phoenix. Nuclear sclerosis causes a blue tint in the lens of the eye but does not affect vision the same way cataracts do, and it is slower in progression. The effect this seems to have on Nigel appears to be his inability to judge distance or depth with a great deal of accuracy. I have also noticed that Nigel's peripheral vision is lacking, and he startles easily if I approach him from the side. I always make sure he is aware of my presence before touching him.

Keep in mind that a dog with compromised eyesight may unintentionally nip your hand as you feed him a treat. If this happens, set yourself up for success by placing his treats on his feeding mat, or feed them to him from the palm of your hand instead of your fingers.

Dental problems

Just as you did when your dog was young, continue those good habits of brushing his teeth to help avoid the necessity of a dental procedure that requires anesthesia. Clean teeth are less likely to spread harmful bacteria throughout the body, which can affect organ systems. I still brush Nigel's teeth every day. This is a habit I got into when he was a pup, and both he and Divot always seemed to enjoy it. A few pieces of carrot afterward was their reward. Nigel can no longer chew bully sticks due to his weakened front paw, so each day I put yogurt in a Kong toy and freeze it for him. This at least gives him something to do and to chew on. *Sort* of.

Digestive Issues/Incontinence/House soiling

As your Norwich ages, his digestive system may become more sensitive. What he used to be able to eat, may now give him loose stools, diarrhea, or gas. Your elderly dog may even lose some of his sense of smell and taste and thus his appetite may diminish. Some claim that older dogs should be given a lower protein food because they do not need protein for building muscle. It has been suggested that a high protein diet is harder for an older dog to digest, resulting in loose stools, gas, etc. Others believe that no change in diet is required for the aging dog. Dr. Bryan emphasizes, "All dogs are individuals and may need a diet tailored to their specific needs. In my opinion, there is no 'one best' food that fits every dog's needs." Dr. Bryan and I agree that it is best to feed your dog what he does well on.

The elderly dog may begin to experience incontinence. There are several things that could cause this problem. First you will want to rule out serious concerns such as infection, bladder stones, cancer, etc. When disease or serious illness is ruled out, incontinence is often found to be caused by a spay or neuter procedure, pain, cognitive dysfunction, or the fact that he is old and just lacks the strength to hold his bladder like he used to. When Divot was about five years old she began to leak urine in her sleep. After a thorough examination and tests ruled out illness, it was determined that incontinence was the result of weakened muscles, a somewhat common problem that can follow a spay procedure. I decided to try a natural remedy called a glandular, coupled with a homeopathic remedy, and it was very effective in stopping Divot's leakage throughout the rest of her life. There are also pharmaceuticals that your vet can prescribe for those who prefer to go that route. See what works best for *your* dog.

If your dog is suffering from cognitive decline he may begin to soil in the house. He may not relieve himself when you take him out and instead, may do so when you bring him back in. He is confused and may not even know he is doing it. Some dogs seem to show awareness of the mistake and act "embarrassed" or "sorry." Never scold him for this – he cannot help it! This is not a time for reprimands. It is instead a time for the utmost patience, compassion, and understanding. Clean the spot thoroughly and move on. If necessary, there are belly bands for boys and panties for girls. These products will protect your home and furnishings, and using them means your old friend will not have to be banished from the family, spending his twilight years alone in another room.

Skin & Coat

As they age, some Norwich begin to show discomfort with the stripping process. I believe that the reason is because skin loses its elasticity and thus the pulling of the coat becomes painful for them. When my dogs showed signs of discomfort, I stopped stripping them and found alternatives to keep their coats tidy. There is no set time that this can or will occur but for us it was around the age of nine for Divot and around 10 for Nigel. Eventually I resorted to clipping their coats. While clipping the coat causes significant shedding, comfort for our elderly dogs outweighs their appearance and our convenience.

Run your hands over your dog on a regular basis. You may find new bumps and lumps on your aging dog. Most of these will be benign little eruptions but be sure to make them known to your vet in case there is something unusual going on. Be sure you are gently brushing your senior dog daily if he seems comfortable with it. This will help with circulation, will eliminate some shedding, will scratch hard-to-get-to places, and probably feel really good.

Cognitive Deficiencies - Difficulty Understanding and Personality Changes

You may begin to notice personality changes in your elderly Norwich. Maybe he no longer tolerates being groomed, mentally *or* physically. Maybe he does not want to be petted as much as he used to, perhaps he prefers to go off alone to sleep without interruption, or does not get up to follow you from room to room like he used to. These things are not out of the ordinary in an elderly dog, but beyond that, it could be something more than just old age.

Canine Cognitive Dysfunction (CCD) is a sort of dementia in dogs and does not have an underlying physical cause – it is a decline in cognitive ability. Some common signs that your dog might be experiencing cognitive decline are:

- Seems lost, even in his own house and/or yard.
- Wanders aimlessly, and paces.
- Sleep patterns change radically. He sleeps all day and paces all night.
- Goes to the wrong side of the door.
- Gets "stuck" in a corner or against a wall.
- Has difficulty understanding instruction.
- Stares into space.
- Barks or whines for no reason.
- Stops signaling the need to go out.
- Soils in the house.

- Withdraws from family, does not recognize family members.

Nigel has begun to display many of these difficulties. It began with him going to the wrong side of the door, unable to understand that the other side was wide open, and has escalated from there. He has become silent for the most part, and no longer signals us to indicate that he needs to go out. In fact, he rarely makes any sound at all anymore. Even the dreams of his youth, once vocal and active, have ceased. He is now silent even in his dreams.

He has begun to soil in the house. Sometimes he gets to the threshold of the door and goes on the rug, or will not eliminate outside and will go instead, when we come back in. Since he no longer signals his need to go out, we make a point of taking him out every few hours to help avoid these kinds of mistakes. At first he seemed to be surprised by his actions, but as the dementia has progressed, he no longer understands that he is soiling his own home. After being such a reliable dog his whole adult life, sadly, the dementia seems to have erased his instinct to be clean.

He tends to wander and pace in the morning and evening, and lately he seems to have great difficulty in understanding simple instruction. He is not always comfortable being petted and often prefers to just be *near* me instead. Nigel sometimes seems very confused upon waking so I allow him to fully awaken before I touch him.

There are products available both natural and pharmaceutical, that claim to help improve cognitive abilities in dogs. Discuss your concerns with your vet and find out what success, if any, he or she has had in other patients using these drugs or natural remedies. Barring any negative side effects, it may not hurt to try. With Nigel, I have begun to do what I call "playing mind games." I put a piece of food somewhere on his feeding mat in the kitchen. While I am working in the kitchen I tell him to, "Go find it!" He must use his nose to find the treat. He generally knows where the treat will be but even so, it can sometimes take him a while to find it. Is it working to sharpen his mind? I really don't know but it cannot hurt to have him learn to rely more on his nose, and focus on a task.

This time in your dog's life is not without trials but with your perseverance, compassion, flexibility, and creativity, you and your dog can work though these difficulties and you both can still enjoy and treasure these very special, very golden years.

When Is The Right Time to Say Good-bye?

Unfortunately for us, letting our beloved Divot go was a decision that was made for us by her ongoing, worsening seizures. That terrible morning we questioned whether it was right to ask her to endure more seizures while we continued to try medication combinations, not even knowing if they would work. We both agreed that neither of us would wish to suffer in such a way, nor would we want that for each other. We knew that we had to let her go because her quality of life had become very low quality. Divot deserved better.

For most dog owners however, the decision may be a long and gut-wrenching process of asking yourself *"Is it time?"* This is a process that I do not have experience with but it is something that Dr. Bryan and I have discussed. He tells me, "When to euthanize is possibly the most difficult decision many owners face. All cases are not clear-cut. I recommend that owners ask themselves, *'Would I want to live in this condition?'* When the answer is 'no,' then it is time to let go." He continues, "The biggest regret I hear repeatedly is, *'I waited too long to euthanize.'* Owners must do what is best for their dog and put aside *their* wants and emotions. I believe that it is our responsibility as owners in return for the unconditional love our dogs give us." He ends our conversation with his favorite quote (author unknown): *"Love him like he's yours forever and he'll be just around the corner."*

Words to love and to live by indeed.

A NORWICH TALE

A Tender Tale of Time – May 2011

Coming Full Circle.

As I write this tale for the last chapter of Norwich Tales, it is a beautiful spring morning in North Carolina. It is the kind of morning that is so perfect in temperature and beauty, one is driven to go outside and do *something*. The spring bulbs have already come and gone, and the perennials are now staking their claim in the landscape, as are the annuals I planted a week ago. The grass is damp with dew and there is an earthy smell in the air with a hint of rosemary and honeysuckle. The sound-track to this perfect morning is the sweet sound of songbird twitter from a chorus of Chickadees, Carolina Wrens, and Finches. As I emerge from the house, Canadian Geese fly overhead as they do every morning on their way from one pond to another. Their loud honks echo as they pass, and as I look up, the morning sun is casting a golden glow upon their bellies. These are the sights, sounds, and smells of our home and I hope never to leave this beautiful place.

As I walk through the dewy yard this morning pondering how I might end this book – this sometimes very painful journey – I am picking up seedpods from the Sweetgum tree that continuously litters our yard throughout the spring. These pods resemble a weapon used in medieval times – a spiked iron ball, or mace, as some would call it. If you step on one of these pods in your bare feet, it feels like a weapon too. Accompanying me as I work is Nigel. He is an old dog now, and as he ambles slowly next to me, he occasionally thrusts his nose into my hand, to see if I have decided to harvest something edible for him, rather than these silly pods I am putting in my bucket. As I look at him I cannot help but feel a sense of pride along with a tinge of sadness.

He is like an old soldier – still tough, and still proud and sometimes my attempts to help him are met with resistance and even protest. He does not want my help as much as he wants his dignity. But the battles he has fought and the injuries he has sustained have left their scars. He is a little slow getting around now, and his mind is not always clear. At times he seems very confused, while at other times he appears to be quite lucid. The dementia is progressing, and just as in humans, it is a cruel fate for such an intelligent, once vibrant being, who was an amazing problem solver. He no longer understands play or displays his delightful sense of humor. He has even completely forgotten the name of his cherished friend Divot, and shows no reaction when her name is spoken. Whether this is the dementia or a natural progression for a dog, I do not know. To Nigel, Divot is not even a memory. To him, she never existed.

He is a little tank though, and keeps rolling forward, seemingly unstoppable, seemingly defiant. Lately, though old age and some of his maladies have made him feel a little vulnerable and my once independent dog does not stray far from me, especially when we are outside. After 13 years of going for a daily walk, Nigel refuses to leave his yard, and now prefers to amble slowly around his own yard for his outings. He is a homebody once again.

My handsome old friend – we have come full circle.

Nigel seems more needy these days, not that he wants to be held or even petted so much, but he just seems to need to be near me. Perhaps it was the devastating loss of our dearest friend and our mutual grief that brought him near again. For so long Mike was Nigel's "special person" but now he is my constant companion again, getting up to follow me if I leave the room, spending his days sleeping in my office, lying at my feet in the evening, and sleeping next to my side of the bed at night. Maybe he senses the sadness I still feel after losing Divot. Maybe, just as he sensed an unsaid need in his little friend Justin so many years ago, he does the only thing he knows how to do – he offers himself as comfort.

We have been through so many changes in these 13 years, and here we are still changing, still learning, and still facing new challenges; all of us older, and all of us a bit wiser. We have come a long way from the well intentioned but ignorant people we were when we brought Nigel home. We probably made his formative years more difficult than they needed to be, but we learned and we committed to changing our way of thinking and our way of *being* in order to give him and Divot what they needed to be fulfilled and happy dogs. I still have to fight my human urge to hug Nigel and hold him close – affectionate overtures that are offensive to him. Instead, I gently pet him or scratch his chin or rump. *That* is what he enjoys.

We have come full circle, and it is just the three of us again. As we amble along, my mind weaves through the past, comes back to the present, and looks to the future...

I have heard it said, "You don't get the dog you *want*, you get the dog you *need*."[1] I was fortunate to get both. I started my search 17 years ago for the perfect dog. Once I got him, it was not as easy or picture perfect as expected. We were two different species sharing a home, with neither understanding each other's language. At times it was difficult and frustrating for both of us, but the more I learned about the nature of dogs, the more successful our relationship became. As it turns out, I did get the perfect dog for me – *the dog I needed.* Nigel taught me about patience, to think "outside the box," and to never give up when something is worth working for. He has certainly taught me to be as tenacious as any terrier! For all the things I wanted to change about Nigel, in the end, it is I who changed the most. He simply adapted to my changes.

Then there was Divot, my special and dear little friend. Divot was such an easy dog to live with, and the most affectionate, adaptable and trusting dog I have ever known. Divot taught me about leadership by watching her consistent confidence with other dogs. With Divot I experienced a particularly unique and special bond between a human and a dog. She was *the dog I always wanted*, and the *other* perfect dog for me. I was fortunate to have known her, to learn from her, and to have shared more than nine wonderful years of my life with her. We did not get to see Divot grow old like Nigel has and I often wonder, if the seizures hadn't started, how she might have naturally aged.

As for the future? Well-intentioned people have asked, "Will you replace Divot?" *Replace her?* I know they mean well so I don't get hung up on the semantics. Some suggest that I "get a new friend for Nigel," but he would not be happy with another dog in his life, certainly not at this stage. It is my duty and responsibility to make sure that his remaining years are enjoyable and peaceful. For now, seeing Nigel through this phase is the most important thing to me. Besides, he and I both know that Divot was the only dog for him.

I know that I will always have a Norwich Terrier in my life, and someday when the time is right, we will have another puppy to love, and we will put all that we have learned into raising that new puppy. He or she will be as precious, unique, and special as Nigel and Divot, and will bring his or her own special meaning to our lives, leaving an indelible stamp on our hearts, as only a Norwich Terrier can do. Just as Nigel and Divot have done.

As I return from my momentary reverie of what was and what will be, I can't help but smile at my handsome little friend who is ambling along beside me this present morning. "Come on old boy" I say. When he looks up at me, his mouth is relaxed and open and it appears that he is smiling. I can only wonder what other lessons he, my most determined teacher, has yet to teach me.

PUPPY NEEDS LIST

- Small crate.
- Food and water bowls – I recommend stainless steel, preferably with nonskid bottom.
- Leash and collar – adjustable collar grows with your pup. I recommend a 4' leash.
- Food – ask breeder what puppy is currently being fed. If you change foods, do so very slowly.
- Absorbent training pads – if you are "paper training."
- Chew toys – if you do not give him something to chew, he'll find something to chew.
- Play toys – soft, silly things that squeak. Dogs love them.
- Treats – for training. Use something small and healthy such as Cheerios.
- Baby gate or X-pen – you will want to limit his ability to roam until he's housebroken.
- Brush & comb.
- Stripping tools – ask your breeder to recommend and demonstrate use.
- R-7 Ear Powder – dabbing fingers in rosin helps grip hair for stripping.
- Nail clippers or rotary tool (such as Dremel) – the latter gets my vote for ease and safety of trimming nails.

- Toothbrush and toothpaste – buy toothpaste specifically made for dogs.

- Shampoo – ask breeder what he or she recommends.

- Small rounded scissors – to trim the hair around foot pads.

- Bitter Apple Cream – can be used on lamp cords, finished wood furniture, etc., to deter chewing.

This list will get you started. You will discover more things you need as time goes by.

ENDNOTES

Chapter 1

[1] The Official Norwich Terrier Breed Standard, Norwich Terrier Club of America (NTCA), www.norwichterrierclub.org

[2] Magda Omansky, *Anatomy of Upper Airway Syndrome*, Norwich Terrier Club of America, www.norwichterrierclub.org

[3] Linda Haring, *Canine Epilepsy*, Norwich Terrier Club of America (NTCA), www.norwichterrierclub.org

[4] Magda Omansky, *What's the Deal With Health Testing?*, Norwich Terrier Club of America (NTCA), www.norwichterrierclub.org

Chapter 3

[1] ASPCA http://www.aspca.org

[2] US Department of Agriculture Audit Report 33002-4SF May 2010

Chapter 5

[1] Ch. Chidley Willum the Conquerer, bred by Karen Anderson, owned by Ruth Cooper and Patricia P. Lussier

Chapter 8

[1] Patricia McConnell, PH.D., The Other End of the Leash. Random House Ballentine Publishing Group. Copyright © 2002 by Patricia B. McConnell, Ph.D. Pages 16-17.

Chapter 12

[1] Michael Podell MSc,DVM Diplomate ACVIM (Neurology), Chicago, IL, http://www.michaelpodelldvm.com/EPILEPSY.html Copyright 2007-2011. Dr. Michael Podell. As quoted, October 2010.

Chapter 12 (continued)

[2] Dr. Robert Bergman DVM, MS, Diplomate, ACVIM (Neurology), Carolina Veterinary Specialists

Chapter 15

[1] Cesar Millan, The Dog Whisperer, The National Geographic Channel

RESOURCES

American Animal Hospital Association, (AAHA),
http://www.aahanet.org

American Holistic Veterinary Medical Association (AHVMA),
http://www.ahvma.org

American College of Veterinary Internal Medicine, (ACVIM),
http://www.acvim.org

Norwich Terrier Club of America (NTCA),
http://norwichterrierclub.org

American Kennel Club, (AKC),
http://www.akc.org

Canine Eye Registration Foundation (CERF),
http://www.vmdb.org/cerf.html

Orthopedic Foundation for Animals (OFA),
http://www.offa.org/

Canine Health Information Center (CHIC),
http://www.caninehealthinfo.org/

Yahoo Norwich Terrier Group,
http://pets.groups.yahoo.com/group/NorwichTerrier/

Marina Zacharias – Natural Rearing,
http://www.naturalrearing.com

NOTE: At the time of this printing, all links are accurate. Visit primary website for updated information.

ABOUT THE AUTHOR

Barbara Huffman is the founder of Norwichtales.com, a popular website with Norwich Terrier enthusiasts since 2002. Many Norwich Terrier breeders make her website a "must read" for prospective puppy buyers. While fascinated with the study of canine behavior, her expertise lies in the everyday living with and loving of the Norwich Terrier. Barbara is co-owner of Huffman Media with her husband Michael, and is the Communications Director at a Charlotte based firm. The Huffman's live in a suburb of Charlotte, NC with their elderly gentleman Norwich Terrier, Nigel.

Printed in Great Britain
by Amazon

70794902R00135